Julie Armstrong is a writer, educator, yogini and lover of wild things. Her writing has been published by Crocus Books, Bloomsbury, Palgrave Macmillan, Little Toller and the Guardian's Country Diary. She has an MA in Writing Studies and a PhD in Creative Writing.

Also, by Julie Armstrong

Mirror Cities

Dream Space

THE MAGIC OF WILD THINGS

Julie Armstrong

ISBN: 979 8554346 828

Cover design and illustration © David Colton

Moonflower Press

moonflower@btinternet.com
Typeset in Century 11pt by Moonflower Press, England.

For Callum & Emme, with love

'So it is time for a new story, a new myth, a change of mindset, attitude and behaviour. If we feel it, we must be galvanized by our ecological grief.'

Lucy Jones: *Losing Eden, Why Our Minds Need The Wild, 2020.*

' "Ki" to signify a being of the living Earth. Not "he" or "she", but "ki". So that when we speak of Sugar Maple, we say, "Oh that beautiful tree, ki is giving us sap again this spring." And we'll need a plural pronoun, too, for those Earth beings. Let's make this new pronoun "kin". So, we can now refer to birds and trees, not as things, but as our earthly relatives. On a crisp October morning we can look up at the geese and say, "Look, kin are flying south for the winter. Come back soon."

Language can be a tool for cultural transformation. Make no mistake: "Ki" and "kin" are revolutionary pronouns. Words have power to shape our thoughts and our actions. On behalf

of the living world, let us learn the grammar of animacy. We can keep "it" to speak of bulldozers and paperclips, but every time we say "ki," let our words reaffirm our respect and kinship with the more-than-human world. Let us speak of the beings of Earth as the "kin" they are.'

Professor Robin Wall Kimmerer: *Grammar Of Animacy.*

Yes Magazine, Spring, 2015: Nature Needs A New Pronoun To Stop The Age Of Extinction, Let's Start by Ditching 'It'.

Hamsa Mantra: aham ('I am') sah ('that')
Hamsa means swan and is a metaphor for the inner self (atman) and also for the breath (prana). This mantra reveals the true nature of the self.

A true self is in everyone, like the scent of a flower, like butter in milk, like oil in sesame seeds, gold in ore, or a thread (strung) through beads. (*Dhyanabindu Upanishad, Verse 5*)

FOREWORD

I am deeply humbled to have been asked to write the foreword for this beautiful book; although magick and wild things are two of my favorite things, so, it is apt. The novella sang a song directly to my heart. I read it in amazement, joy and sadness. I read it with love shimmering in my heart and love beamed back at me from every page. It is the kind of book you can read over and over again, as it reveals new levels, more truths and insights with each revisit. I wanted to start it again the moment I'd finished it, knowing already that even though I'd been completely transfixed, it still had more to offer and I could go even deeper in.

This is a work of heartfelt passion. It is like a poem that continues to unfold, rolling onwards as the seasons turn. I felt I'd been lifted up and transported to a sacred space, in between worlds, in between times. I lay against a mossy stone as I read, in the clearing of a wild and ancient wood.

The small, stone cottage just down the path, its windows warmed by soft firelight. A great canopy of green reached above my head, affording only glimpses of sky. I had slipped through a portal and dropped right into a magickal fairytale. Birdsong sings from these pages. I felt the powerful beating of a swan's wings fan my skin and the magick of moonlight illuminated the trees. I could smell the deep earthy aroma of a forest floor, feel the green, the life, and the crunch of leaves beneath me.

I knew nature in all her forms, how it was to fly like a bird, and to bask in the deep rootedness of a tree. I felt my skin as bark, caressed by soft lichen, and knew the quiet gentle sadness of death and decay. I saw the world through the eyes of a vixen, while at the same time being in awe of the sun lighting the golden russet richness of her fur.

There are human stories here too, a romantic love, a child's love, a mother's love, and a love of the natural world; separate yet cleverly woven as one. When I'd finished reading, I had to go outside and sit in the garden for a while, to let myself gently return from cloud walking. And it was then that I realized this story is also a prayer, about, and from, the earth itself.

It is outside time. It speaks of the past, present and the future. That said, it is without question also a book OF our time. We need these stories now.

I am an artist, a writer, and a witch of the old ways, of natural magick. I've been watching the world turn my whole life with a breaking heart. My activism shifting eventually from a blaze of banner waving rage, chaining myself to things, to gentle deep prayer and loving, insightful intention. In all I do it is my profound wish to connect people to their own hearts, and in doing so, to connect them to the heartbeat of the very planet we live on. Awakening humanity to the knowledge that there is no separation between us and Gaia. That we are one.

In all of my work, I invite people to really

experience the beauty and magick of the natural world, to respect it, move fluidly with the natural cycles, to honor our place in it. As I see it this is our salvation.

I believe this magickal book is part of this awakening. I'd challenge anyone to read this and not be moved by it, transformed even. Our natural world is described from such a sacred knowing, that it must surely melt the hardest heart, and inspire the softest. And this is the power of it, that it opens our hearts, eyes to a love of simple, yet magickal, things. A walk in the woods becoming a journey into a fairytale. Our world today is shaking, shifting, burning, flooding and weeping. It is poisoned, damaged, abused and brutalized. The creatures we share this planet with are suffering, really suffering, at human hands. Great swathes of natural landscapes all over the world, habitats and homes for the feathered, furred and winged ones, the scaly beings, insect life and all our swimming brethren are destroyed daily, and for what, progress?

Human consumption, avarice, greed, corruption and a lack of care, plus, human disconnect on a grand scale are all creating a toxic situation globally, that ultimately affects us all, affects everything. We cannot escape or pretend it's not us, it's them. We all have a part to play.

We are heading full pelt and blindly to our own destruction. And that of others, those innocent beings who still live rightly and lightly on the land, in the skies and the sacred waters.

The tipping point is here, many species are already extinct. Others hanging on by a thread; it's barely believable to me that it's got this out of hand. Humanity is at a crossroads, and we as conscious individuals have to make a choice.

Love needs to save the day.

This novella is a tale of love, at its heart a love of the natural world. It is an honoring. And the sacred truths written here will, I am sure, weave their beautiful sparkling magick into the hearts of all that are blessed to read it.

As I said, I am humbled to have been asked to write this foreword. It is my great blessing in this life to have been gifted with a great love of nature and all the creatures we share our world with. It's a way of being that brings much joy and solace.

To have played a small part in this sacred truth coming into the world, this heart song for the magickal wild ones fills me with deep humility, and hope for the future.

Please, let your heart fill with its beauty, and share it with everyone you know, the ocean is after all made of many little drops.

Much love, and Blessed Be.

Jo Thilwind, Dreamspace, Cheshire, England, planet Earth, 2020 x

SMALL, STONE COTTAGE

Bel, do you remember what happened? After all
it was a long time ago. You were only a pollen-
speck of a girl, golden and tiny. So, you may
have forgotten? Though Jack said I wasn't
myself, I'm still crushed by guilt. You see, I'd
slipped between cracks into other worlds, but
believe me, when I tell you, the events I'm going
to share are true. At least I think they are,
memory plays tricks. It was a terrifying time.
We were cursed. As much as I tried, there was
nothing I could have done to prevent it. Even
now I'm not sure where to start, I suppose, at the
beginning, the morning of the spring equinox.

Coming behind me, his hand on my back, Jack
saw me packing my rucksack. I squealed like a
rabbit caught in a trap. You were by his side,
soft and rosy, jaw slack, just out of bed. Hair like
a dandelion clock.
'What are you doing?' he asked, leaf litter lifting

in his throat.

Cold clamminess crept over my scalp. 'I'm sorry, Jack, but I can't stay in the city any longer.'

'You're leaving?'

'It isn't like that.'

Weather-worn, dark-bark skin. 'How is it then?'

'I'm unhappy. This isn't the life for me.'

You did not make a sound as he took hold of your small, star-shaped hand, just stared at me with forget-me-not blue eyes.

He waved his branches. 'What about us?'

A rush of shame. Although anger stirred in my belly too. My head boiling like a witch's brew.

'I know I'm your wife, but I belong to me.' I sighed. 'I've lost my stories.'

He nodded, slowly.

'I miss the wild so much, don't you?'

I think I heard him sigh and rustle. 'You know I do.'

He lived in the forest when I met him, just after I'd escaped from that hell hole. I can't speak about that now. Maybe later.

'We were happy living in the forest, weren't we?'
There was a sound like the felling of trees. 'The
lungs of planet Earth,' he wheezed.

I agreed, thinking of the time Jack and I made
tonic out of sap, used bark to ease pain. Saying
'thank you,' again and again to show our
appreciation. As the trees shed their branches,
twigs and leaves, to provide nourishment for the
saplings. Until the workmen arrived, wearing
florescent orange jackets and hard, white hats
brandishing chainsaws as weapons. Jack cried,
'Trees have the same rights as us!'
But they did not listen.

He planted himself in front of me. 'I can't live
without you, May. Please, stay.'
I threw my arms in the air. 'How can I? The city
is killing me. I want to live in the place of my
dreams.'
I'd told Jack how each night my consciousness
slipped its mooring, drifted over a land steeped

in folklore to a small, stone cottage where I had
to be with living things, watching them grow.
But he ignored me. You gave me a sideways
look. What were you thinking? Shyly, you held
out your other hand. I took it. You pressed it to
your lips, kissed it.

'Maybe it's not a dream but a memory, Mammy?'
I felt lightheaded. Did you really say that? Wise
child. I smiled. 'Maybe Sweet pea.' Then I
turned my attention to Jack. 'I have to go there.
Try and understand, my love. It's where my true
self should be. I have a feeling there's something
waiting there for me.'

'Let's all go then,' he announced suddenly.
The air went out of the city. 'Really? You'll do
that for me?'

He swayed, but was earthbound, so much below
ground. 'I don't want to lose you.'

I put my arms on his girth. His long tendrils of
tree ferns tickled my face as I kissed him. His
scent-sunshine warming the earth-promise of our
rebirth.

18

'I don't want to lose you either.'

And I didn't, not then, not ever, nor you, but some things are unstoppable, aren't they, despite what we do? Yet, I have never got over what happened. I never will. Do you believe me, Bel? I hope so.

Did I tell you that Mother was a story-teller like me? Probably not. I rarely spoke about Mother, did I? Yet, now it's time to weave my memories into the fabric of your life, including the stories she told me. Stories of the natural world, some I told you. Do you remember them, Bel?

I imagine you do. Tucked up in bed you listened, not making a sound, spell bound.

'One more,' you said. 'I'm one more hungry.'

And I laughed. It was such a quirky thing to say, wasn't it? But you were always saying quirky things. You were a quirky little girl. And I thought I understood you. But I didn't, did I? I did later when the awful thing happened.

Let me tell you what Mother was like. She was tall as the mountain, deep as the river, ageless as starlight. Silver hair rushed down her back. Copper rings on her fingers and toes, one through her nose, bracelets on her arms. Her flowing robes from another age, dyed with the plants growing in the forest. She sang to the trees.

'Magic is a conversation with the natural world,' she often said to me, running her long fingers through my hair.

Mother told the most enchanting stories. Sit bones rooted into the earth, cross-legged, hands held softly in her lap. Me by her side, sitting round the fire along with the villagers who all came to listen. There was the miller, the gravedigger, the candle stick maker. There were beekeepers, weavers, knitters and spinners, all waiting patiently for her to begin.

'Stories are a form of alchemy,' she said. Flames leaping in her eyes as she threw elder twigs into

the fire. There was a roaring and a crackling. 'If we imagine another world we can create it.'
We held our breath, willing her to say more. And when she did, it was as if she had opened a door, into a garden sparkling and glittering with gems.

Mother spun stories all night, twisting tales, pulling the yarn of her words tight. Until the moon sliced to lemon, then ghosted away, as the orange sun rose through veils of mist. And silhouettes of hares appeared boxing on Seven Stars Hills.

Do you remember us leaving the city, Bel? We were full of hope for change, weren't we?
Trundling back in time, to a place of open fields and vast skies. Driving with the windows down, I felt myself coming alive. A breeze sopping sweetly, smelling of wildflowers and the tang of rising sap. Everywhere a luminescent green. Flashing through the forest, we heard the trees exhaling oxygen. And there were insect ticks and

mossy sighs, whispering leaves, hot breath of
bracken, animal bones clacking, feathers
flapping. Twisting roots shouting to shoots
pushing into the world with ear piercing cries.
'A wise-woman lives in the forest,' I said to you.
'I know she does, Mammy. I saw her.'
And I believed you.
'Spring is a time of promise,' I said to Jack.
He smiled, took one hand from the steering
wheel, ran it up and down my back: 'I know that.'
I smiled too. 'I know you do.'
'Everything is aware and awake.'
So many treasures,' I said to you, pointing at the
waysides bright-eyed with speedwell.
'Your little face lit up like a lantern. 'I love them.
They are family.'

The ditches were embroidered with dog violets
and cowslips, primroses and stitchwort, coltsfoot,
pink campion, buttercups and daisies.
Dandelions stood bold as brass in the grass.
Celandines too, gold sequins stitched along lanes

buzzing with bees. Swallows bright as needles pierced the sky. Butterflies flickering in rainbow-patterns of themselves: silver spotted-skipper, orange-tips, chalk hill blue. Wild orchids too. Long tailed tits singing like tiny bells ringing. Red squirrels leaping from tree to tree with glee. Hawthorn hedges thronged with sparrows and thrushes, blackbirds and robins, whistling a recipe of earthworms and woodlice. Tiny footprints of mice. Otters and badgers. Rabbits and adders. A herd of deer suddenly rose out of the mist then disappeared like an apparition. And I felt such a deep calm and joy being with the magic of wild things.

A bursting of buds as Jack looked briefly into my eyes. And at that moment, I could not have loved him more if I'd tried. I recall him once saying,
'My love for you is etched into my rings.'
When I told you that, you smiled: remember?
Jack was the best of men, wasn't he? A

wonderful partner, a kind and protective father.
Mother never spoke about mine. And I never
asked. Why would I? I imagine, I inherited his
flaming red hair and green eyes, but I had no
desire to know about him. And didn't bother to
listen to the villagers' tittle tattle saying he
wasn't quite human. Mother filled my life with
light. I didn't need anyone else. Until I lost her.
We drove over a rickety bridge. Below, the river-
that-runs-both-ways was rushing and frothing,
slurping and gurgling, spitting at briars, licking
ripe and rot, gobbling green snot, twirling,
swirling in a dance of its own making.

Wood anemones opened their pristine white faces
to the sky, smiling as we drove by. A misting
lisping violet-blue, patterns of bark and bent
twigs, soft sounds of lichen and cloud shapes
shifting, wild garlic hissing too: the landscape's
language. Such a sense of belonging. We were
too full to talk.

Out of the corner of my eye, I caught a glitter of orange and blue, turquoise too, an arrow of jewels flying swiftly through shafts of gold. Folklore has it that if a dead kingfisher is hung by twine, it acts as a weather cock, always turning its beak in the direction of the wind, but I imagine you know that already, Bel, don't you?

The wise-woman was fishing. She wore earth-brown skirts and big boots. Eyes the colour of vines. Face wrinkled as a pickled walnut. She raised her hand in greeting. I did the same. Did she know me from another life?

Puttering up a hill, passing a cluster of stone cottages, charcoal lines of smoke drawn from chimneys to the sky. Air pungent with woodsmoke. You croaked. Turned green as a frog, tiddlywink tiny. Passing a church sculpted from granite. I saw a sheela-na-gig carved over its big wooden door and the face of a Green Man peering out from the porch.

The lanes were narrower now. We stopped
briefly at the edge of a lake. Guarded by tall
pines, nodding at us. A wild swan glided over
the water one leg tucked onto its back. Lifting
its head to the sky:
aham sah aham sah
You smiled, didn't you?

The ancient track was overhung with hazel trees,
knotted with ivy, casting shadows over our faces.
Bumping alongside the stream, speaking in light
and shade, remembering a future that had
already happened. Jack rubbed his eyes. The
backs of his hands networked with ley lines.
'Are we going the right way?' he asked.
There was no map, but instinctively I knew.
'Yes, not far now.' I rubbed my hand gently up
and down his knee. 'Thank you so much for
making this journey with me.'

The front wheels spun over grass as Jack turned

the truck round a bend. Compost and seeds everywhere. Into the distance I stared, balling my fists in excitement. As it was there, coming close, partially hidden by tall grass and brambles the small, stone cottage of my dreams.

Jack cut the engine, it sparked and blew, bits of deep-blue sky in his right eye. Momentarily we just sat there. Then I flung open the door, scrambled out of the truck and pushed open the wooden gates, creaking and grating on rusty hinges. As I crossed the threshold something shifted in me as I slipped into another reality. Do you remember, Bel, there was the most amazing energy? My whole body was singing. 'I'm so alive!' I cried. As I felt myself re-rooting into the earth, re-aligning with nature's rhythms.

I found a thick stick near a silver birch tree and hacked through the brambles.

'New beginnings,' I called to Jack, who was
giving you a piggyback. Swiping at the tall grass,
beating a path to the front door. Hands beaded
with blood; I did not care. The words over and
over in my head: I am home!

Bel, do you remember our small, stone cottage?
The three stone steps leading up to the door
worn with footfalls. The downstairs windows
laced with cobwebs. I rubbed one and peered
inside. There was no surprise. It was exactly as
I knew it would be. Leaning walls, sloping,
beamed ceiling, uneven stone-flagged floor.
Copper pots and pans hanging from hooks. The
broom made from twigs against a whitewashed
wall, galvanized pails and a wicker basket with
pegs. There was the deep, stone sink with one
tap. A pair of muddy boots on the mat. The hat
and coat stand draped with a long, black, woolen
coat. A dresser next to a wooden ladder leading
to the bedrooms and attic. I was ecstatic as I

stepped aside to let Jack see. You were snuggled in his arms. Thumb plugged in your mouth. He lifted you higher than the clouds. Immediately your little face lit up again. You turned to me. 'We're home, Mammy.'

My heart beat a strange rhythm. 'Yes, we are, Sweet pea.'

Jack whistled a verdant tune, trailing ivy, swaying slightly. And I heard it again in the distance:

aham sah aham sah

I squinted through the next window. Inside it was furnished with recycled things. Rough, hewn planks propped between ladders teetering either side one wall, stacked with old books. Black, rustic barrels were tables. A chandelier crafted from the front wheel of an old barrow hung from the beamed ceiling. There were wicker chairs with faded cushions. A hearth and mantlepiece fashioned from oak, a wood burner, brass poker and basket of logs. There were candles set in saucers in the windowsill. Coarse hessian sacks spread over the floor. And a handmade wooden door.

I hugged you, kissed Jack. I had not felt like this since I had first met him, did I tell you about that? It was when I had escaped from that hell hole. I wandered into the forest. Far from home. But I was not alone. The trees called softly to me. I smelt their lost words. As the birds settled. And a smear of stars appeared over Seven Stars Hills. The moon, a pearl, glowing on black velvet. There was something else too. A campfire lighting a pocket of sky. Who could it be? I had to go and see. It drew me like a moth to a flame.

You will not believe this, but when I met your father, it was love at first sight. How strange is that? And even stranger, I had loved him before,

I was sure. There was this recognition, you see. It was as if he was part of me. We belonged together. Yet, we had somehow drifted apart. Or had we? He said, he felt the same as me. So, sleeping together that same night felt right. Giving and taking from each other's bodies, lying on our backs. Skying with this ragged man. Breathing in wood smoke. Floating into another world. Listening to distant soft flute sounds. Away with the fauns and faeries. Our union blessing the land's fertility.

We woke muzzy headed from our revelry. Wrapped in each other's arms, lying on the earth, amongst sweetgrass, near the fire's embers, surrounded by roots and shoots. Dirt smutching our faces. Tattoos of sunlight spilling through canopies of oak trees, boughs mossy with age, noisy with rookeries. A tiny bird twittering to and fro. There were twigs and buds in our hair. Spring was in the air. Jack crowned me with a garland of May blossom and called me his queen.

We bathed in the sounds of the lake splashing on rocks and exchanged birch twigs, a symbol of our love. Smiling at each other, both knowing I was seeded with you, hoping we would live happily ever after. If only we knew what was going to happen.

Round the back, the garden was a tangle of knee-high grass and head-high thistles, twitching with butterflies and bees, ticks and flies, buzzing and humming, breeding and hatching. Ladybirds were studded in moss like semi-precious stones. Swallows were building nests, weaving their songs into the eaves. And there were flashes of finches in fruit trees: buttery-bars on their wings, crimson-bloodied faces. Their voices revealing the different personalities of each bird.

Behind the ramshackle shed there were beech trees, percolating sunlight and soil, minerals and rainwater, growing and changing and aging.

Next to a lean-to stacked with logs, there was the
pump which drew its healing water from the well
in Back Field. My feet kissed the earth as I
walked along the path to work its handle.
Nourishing, life-giving water trickled into my
cupped hand; I drank.

And then I smelt it. Nostrils flaring. A stir of
musk on the breeze: glandular, strangely
sensual. Was it coming from me?

I walked to the bottom of the wild garden. She
was there in Back Field, a vixen, the sheen on
her coat was the sun of two summers. Her
amber eyes met mine. The connection passing
between us, so intense, it brought a pain to my
chest. And I recalled something Mother once
said to me.
'An animal can become a human and a human
can become an animal.'
Her words mesmerized me, I believed her, you

see. She was a wise-woman.

Suddenly, the vixen turned and loped away. I
watched her. Staring into the distance at fields
sewn like a quilt from bits of old cloth: bronze,
smudge-brown, coal-black, tattered and stitched
at the edges by hawthorn hedges, patched and
darned in places, falling softly to Green Valley
where mist collected like clotted cream in a deep
bowl. Beyond there was the forest.

In Back Field there was an oak tree stippled with
gold; it waved its boughs at me, bulked into boats
of buds, shining and sailing through the sky. As
I stood beneath it, I returned to my breath,
anchored my mind. Silence rinsing through my
veins like cool rainwater washing me clean.

Jack's footsteps behind me, landing gently as
husks on soft soil, until he was at my side,
holding you close. He gave you to me. I took you

in my arms and whispered in your ear.

'Here you can make friends of the trees, swim
with the river-that-runs-both-ways.

You looked at me quizzically: 'I told you, they are
family.' And you stroked the oak's bark.

But then you said something that shocked me:
'I feel the threat, Mammy, don't you?'

I shook my head. Words stuck at the back of my
throat. Even then you knew what was going to
happen, didn't you?

And yet for three years we lived a meaningful
life, away from the city's strife, in harmony with
all the wildlife. We planted potatoes, tomatoes,
beans and artichokes. Our neighbours were
apple, pear, and plum trees. Days were spent
weeding and watering, nurturing and harvesting.
The food tastier than any we had eaten. We
flourished, brimming with good health.

The small, stone cottage wasn't just home to

Jack, you and me. It was home to so many creatures, wasn't it? It was a living organism, part of the landscape; its beams made from the trees of the forest and the walls built from stone quarried from Seven Stars Hills. Virginia creeper scrambled all over the front walls in which all manner of insects lived. In spring it provided a rich diet for the swallows, when they fed their chicks in mud-cup nests under the eaves, a space they shared with the bats. During the summer months, a variety of butterflies: peacocks, painted ladies, small tortoiseshells, red admirals, alighted on the back walls of the cottage which were encrusted with burnt-orange and pale-grey lichen. They spread their wings in the sun, showing eye spots.

Small green-brown lizards scuttled between cracks in the stones searching for spiders. Moss grew between the slate roof tiles, nourishment for millipedes. And a smooth snake lived in the timbers of the roof space, along with mice, often its food. It was home to a roosting barn owl too, whose pellets were gobbled up by the grubs.

And like the landscape, the small, stone cottage held memories and stories. They echoed in the oak beams and in the stone walls. They scurried in the roof space. Outside they basked on the sun terrace, hid in the wood pile, snoozed in the shed, flew over trees and danced in the breeze. They sheltered in the lean-to and burrowed in the wild garden. And at night, they sparkled like glow worms spangling the earth.

But then on the longest day and shortest night of the fourth year, things started to go wrong ...

MAGPIE

Finishing our celebration feast, nut roast and tomato chutney, we watched the sun set over Seven Stars Hills. You sleeping peacefully on Mother's patchwork blanket, protected by the oak tree's limbs, luxuriating in the shade it gave. Like me, you delighted in the oak tree, didn't you? When I stood beneath it, my emotions soared, so that I often sang and danced. It was a place for you to swing from, climb up, build a den in and camp under. You called it your 'best friend', didn't you? I remember you once saying to me,

'This tree was alive when humans invented writing, Mammy.'

And I believed you.

'Red sky at night, shepherd's delight,' I said to Jack, sipping from my cup of elderberry wine. His eyes glowed gloriously green. As I said, yours were forget-me-not-blue, same shade as

Mother's. It was the first thing I noticed when you slipped from my body wailing and slimy in a whoosh of fluid. I fell into those eyes and drowned. Brow furrowed with soil, rocking on his heels, Jack opened his hands. There were acorns.

'They are a symbol of immortality,' he said, 'but nothing is forever. Everything changes.'

Even though I knew it was true his words knifed my chest. Fleetingly I pulled away, but he was taking something from the top pocket of his branches:

'For you.'

There on the whorls and rings of his palm were two tiny swans on a silver chain which he fastened round my neck.

I fingered the swans at the hollow of my throat, a smile twitching on my lips. His tongue along my collarbone butterfly light. Pulsing with pleasure, I pulled bracken over his head, sank my teeth into his chest, tasting of woodpeckers' beaks, smelling of minerals. The weight of him as he felled me onto my back.

'I love you, Jack.'

And I did, still do.

There was a savage beating of wings. We sat up. Something screeching and dive-bombing, buffeting my back, landing heavily on my head. Open claws digging into my skin, savaging my scalp, pecking my neck. I slumped forward as if I had been shot; it took off, swooping and soaring, tilting and turning, scattering black and white feathers. The two tiny swans and silver chain in its beak. You wide-awake.

'Listen to the universe.' Mother once said to me. 'Take notice of signs and warnings and the prophesy of birds.'

So, at that moment, I was drawn across boundaries into other times, other places. My deepest self-knowing something horrific was going to happen, but I denied it. That is, until spring came.

SNOWDROPS

'Why are you getting up so early?' Jack spoke in
spores, as if he was struggling to free himself
from something. Rolling onto his canopy,
hauling himself up from our carved, wooden bed.
While I slipped into leggings and jumper, pulled
a woolen hat on my head.
'Don't go. Come back to bed.'
'No, Jack.' Lately he was starting to irritate me.
He was so needy. 'I'm going to explore the land
instead.'
'Before it disappears?'
Swinging around hands on hips. A hot prickle on
the back of my neck,
'What do you mean?'
How dare he voice my fears. I wanted to push
him over, but when I moved closer, my heart
sank like a stone to the bottom of my belly.

Jack was scratching his crown. Fingers bent as
twigs. Hands twisted as roots. Nails crawling

with lichen. And he was as bare as winter. His nipples blood-black shriveled buds. His eyes dead wood. Skin parched as withered leaves. Long beard and hair threaded with grey, tangled with last year's nests. Feathers of ice on his nose. The caw of crows. Yawning loudly, his mouth a cave, muddy with earth. Breath mouldy as fungi. My head whirled. The room swirled.

'What's wrong, my love?'

'I feel a thousand years old.'

The day before he had fashioned a hare and crescent moon weathervane from copper. Pulling himself to full height, he fixed it to the roof. The hare leaping towards the late evening sun, glowing like a beacon.

He groaned. 'I'm out of sorts.' My bones feel like mildew and my head's full of lice. I'm going back to sleep. It's not time to wake up.'

'Yes, it is, the light's shifting.'

'Barely.' Then he added: 'Listen.'

'I can't hear anything.'

'Exactly. Where are the birds?' 'In their voices

43

we hear the rhythms of the seasons.'

And with that, he pulled the eiderdown over his head, leaving me with an ache in my chest.

Snowdrops marked the waking of the land from its sleep into new-life, yet that Imbolc I searched and searched, but couldn't find any.

ROBIN

Roaming layers of land, wandering into my imagination, digging deep into memory, I gathered words from beneath stones, plucked calligraphy from old bones, hieroglyphics from dead leaves. I found inspiration in lightning slashes on trees. A single script of bird flight scrawled on the sky. A few footprints of animals trodden into the earth, for me to birth stories. So, that each day, the landscape gifted me, although its gifts that spring were paucity. I didn't know why.

Back at our small, stone cottage, I crept upstairs, so as not to wake you and Jack, to my writing room.

Most days a robin flew in. Landing on the corner of my desk which was piled with books and feathers, pebbles and stones, a sheep's skull, the shell of a wren's egg, dried flowers, acorns, berries, leaves, conkers, tree sap, pinecones and words, all collected on my walks. It had learned to trust me and perched on my hand to peck sunflower seeds from my palm, cocking his head on one side, looking at me through black, beady eyes. Mother once told me.

'The birds watch us as much as we watch them.'

I told you the same thing, do you remember?

Then, when he'd gone, I disappeared into my secret place, my dream space, where: swallows swooped through the skies to find words light as midges landing on dog roses sweet as honeysuckle tumbling over notebooks like freshwater springs full of ideas going with the flow of sentence streams leaping like salmon into paragraphs adders hiding in margins of bracken hedgehogs sleeping in piles of wood shavings from pencil sharp lines of woodsmoke commotions of coots circling in ponds blue as ink blots running with the hare over fields of blank pages filling with fauna and fauna trees losing their leaves flaring into fires of sub plots

finishing with full stops of badger setts and

rabbit burrows

SMOOTH SNAKE

Only two swallows returned in spring. Summer
was wet. And with the dawning of the autumn
equinox, winter arrived like a demon with a knife
at our throats. The leaves did not blaze into
oranges and reds, they simply fell from the trees
instead. There were no rose hips or juicy berries
for the blackbirds and thrushes, no acorns for the
squirrels. No time for migration or hibernation,
lots of creatures dropped down dead. Despite my
hat, the cold hammered nails into my head.

Fat flakes of snow turned the world white
overnight.

One morning, as I was chopping logs, I got a
fright as three spineless hedgehogs hobbled
bloodily along the path. Tears filled my eyes. I
looked to the skies. As if searching for answers,
'What's happened to the poor hedgehogs?'
Jack blistered in blobs of burnt-orange lichen.

Mould sculpted his face out of shape. More and more age rings round his wrists and bird droppings on his cheeks.

'I've seen two dead swallows too,' he said.

Near the hawthorn hedge feathers of scarlet and blue blew in the scalpel slicing wind. The tears rolled down my cheeks.

I carried their brittle bony bodies to the oak tree in Back Field while Jack took a spade from the shed.

Yet, the earth was hard as iron. So, we buried them under piles of leaves. It was then that Jack began to sneeze. Burrs fell from his nose and raindrops that froze. There was the caw of crows as he toppled to a stump in the ground gasping and rasping.

We had not the heart or energy to celebrate Samhain. Jack was bent-double and knotty. For a week, he slept all day and coughed all night. I

49

was so worried, I could not eat or sleep, do you remember that terrible time, Bel? You barely said a word.

A thaw came on the winter solstice swiftly followed by a heat wave at Yule.

The sun blazed for twenty-four hours, for seven days and seven nights from a bright blue, cloudless sky.

Green shoots poked through the ground. Buds opened on slim saplings. Blossom frothed the hedges. Daffodils raised their golden trumpets and blew. Rabbits nibbled celandines, others lay dead in ditches, showing ribs supple as willow. Birds sang all night. But there wasn't a single swallow in sight.

'What's going on, Jack?'

He shrugged the life out of his shoulders. His skin was spongy with moss, scratched by briars. 'What will happen when the weather turns cold again?'

'If it does.'

It did.

After the week of searing heat, more snow
tumbled from the grey laundry sky. Puffy
pillows and fluffy blankets smothering the
hedges and fields.

The landscape was a stopped pocket-watch.

I lit candles, hoping to encourage the return of
the warmth and the light, but each day was long
and cold and dark, same as each night.

Icicles hung like daggers from the eaves of our
small, stone cottage. The pump froze. I had
chilblains. You had cold after cold.

Imbolc came again. I searched alongside the
stream, but I did not find any snowdrops. Only
poison ivy.

For three years around the spring equinox a blue
tit built her nest in a hollow fence post with moss
from the stone wall. She lined it with feathers.
Do you remember? We watched all the chicks
fledge into the hawthorn hedge. But it didn't
happen the fourth year, did it?

There weren't any primroses wandering
wantonly over the fields and into ditches,
delicate lemon petals, egg-yolk centres: *Primula
vulgaris,* Mother's favourite wild flower.

The beast from the east roamed, moaning and
groaning, gnawing our bones.

'What's happened to the primroses and cowslips,
Jack? And the lady's smock? I haven't seen
any in Wild-Flower Field, have you?'
He didn't reply, just wiped the cuckoo spit
streaming from his eye. And nose. His toes
scratching the ground for fossils of what had

been, but not anymore.

The starlings didn't roost in the trees of the wild garden. They squabbled on the roof of our small, stone cottage, like old men, opening their overcoat wings, warming themselves round the chimney pot.

Inside, we kept the fires burning all day and all night. Do you remember the metal pipe that rose from the back of the stove in the living room? It ran up the wall at the back of the chimney breast, warming the stones, travelling into the loft where the smooth snake, wrapped around the timbers, gorged on mice.

One night a stink of rotting meat drifted into our dreams. I sat up in our carved, wooden bed and said, 'Where's that smell coming from, Jack?'

We searched every room of our small, stone cottage.

Then, in the loft, we found it. The smooth snake coiled in a corner decomposing.

The barn owl was nowhere to be found.

Mice littered the ground.

But there was not a single grub to be seen.

SWALLOWS

There were jigsaws of frost on the windows. It
was too cold to undress, so, we wore our clothes
to bed. Hats on our heads, socks on our feet.
'I'm freezing,' I said, teeth chattering like
jackdaws.
Jack pulled me into his nest. 'Things will change
soon.'
And they did the next day, the spring equinox.
We felt it. A profound shift deep in the earth.

Heat beat from a hard-blue sky. We shed our
clothes. Flung the windows and doors open wide.
Stepped outside, then back inside, as clouds of
big bluebottles buzzed into our small, stone
cottage. We closed the windows and doors, but
they swarmed down the chimney.

On the seventh day they all disappeared like a
magic trick.

I imagined the hares boxing. Small, black-topped tails, black-tipped ears, standing on long, hind legs, a doe clouting a buck with her paws, but I did not see them.

And I waited and waited for the swallows to return. I Imagined them flying above sand dunes and mountains, crossing the ocean, finally exploding over the roof of our small, stone cottage in spangles of sunlight and rainbows, arabesques of hope, showing their royal-blue backs and scarlet throats, but I waited in vain, they never came.

One day I found Jack lying on the ground, not making a sound. His face smeared with earth. Fallen branches jutted round his head like horns. His eyes were black twigs. I dropped to his side fearful he'd died. Yet, he held his hands out to me. And I took them. They were furry with frost, mottled with mustard-yellow lichen, pocked with moss, splattered with peat.

'You need to be in bed,' I said.

The skin on his face had a sludgy-green cast. He tried to raise his head, but it was rooted in the ground. Acorns fell from his mouth as he said.

'I feel lifeless, May.'

My heartbeat quickened. The blood rushed through my veins. A rocking sense of vertigo as I helped him to his feet.

'Lean on me.'

And he did. I half-carried, half-dragged him back to our small, stone cottage, up the wooden ladder to our carved, wooden bed where I sat stroking his head.

'Are you feeling any better, my love?'

He nodded. 'A little.'

'Shuffle up. Let me get in with you.'

I snuggled up, holding him close. He was chilled to the roots. So, I gave him a drink of water from the cup on the bedside table. When he was able, he came down the wooden ladder with me for a bowl of broth and a cup of hot, sweet tea. He ate and drank so slowly. A tender, green shoot grew behind his ear. I smiled, but the warm cheer disappeared, when a black thought appeared.

'If swallows don't return yearly to build their nests in the eaves of our small, stone cottage ruin will come to it,' I said.

He dropped his spoon into the bowl. 'I don't believe in folklore anymore.'

'I do, 'I said.

He got up from the table. 'I'm going back to bed.'

STAR FISH & SEA HORSES

'Jack!' I yelled, panic sluicing through me when I
saw them scattered over the bleached grass: star
fish and sea horses: all dead.

He appeared at the back door, bent-double,
coughing. Fungal spores falling from his eyes.
You were at his side sucking your thumb.

'Where's the mermaid?' you said.

'Go back to bed, sleepy-head,' I said.

Unexpectedly, you grabbed my hand and kissed
it.

'I'm kissing you a love heart, Mammy.'

Those were the exact words you said. Love rose
like a wave and broke over me. I picked you up,
crushing you to my chest, thinking if I ever lost
you, I would die.

'I can't breathe,' you gasped.

'Sorry, Bel,' I said, tracing each vertebra of your
back with my fingertips, imagining each one
glowing like white pebbles on the seashore.

You shook your head. 'Words, Mammy.'

'What do you mean, Sweet pea?'

'Words begin with the breath.'

At the time, I had no idea what you meant.

Jack and I made a bonfire and burnt the sea creatures. The air was stinky fishy with smoke. You watched from your bedroom window.

CUCKOO

The following morning, I didn't get up until Jack
did. I lay next to him in a tangle of stifling,
messy sheets as he slept. Listening to the dawn
chorus, heart pitter-pattering in my chest.
Drenched in sweat. A knot pulling taut in my
belly. Mother always said,
'Give the birds your attention and discover the
many messages in their many voices. By
noticing and naming we honour our kinship.'

That year I picked out the song of a blackbird
and robin, but there were no other birds. Once
there had been a symphony of trills and warbles,
coos and whistles.

Later that morning, I said: 'The cuckoo hasn't
returned.'
I was digging over my herb patch. The sun was
blinding. And there was not a breath of wind.
Spilling white berries, Jack disappeared into the

shed, came out blinking, winking at you, a wire brush in his hand.

'I'm worried, Jack. I'm beginning to wonder if the cuckoos and the swallows are extinct; what do you think?'

A crinkling of leaves, so the sun would not burn his neck, spongy with woodworm, pulling branches low over his eyes. He turned his back, puffballs exploding in clouds of brown dust. Fine paint flakes flew into my face as he rubbed frantically at the shed's window frames with the wire brush. They had blistered and scabbed in the heat, like me. Sun scorched skin peeled in sheets.

'I hope not,' he said quietly, planting his feet firmly in the ground.

My heart filled with dread. Even then I knew things would get much worse. It was a feeling I had, dirty, unsettling, like a rat streaking through the shadows of my chest.

'What can we do?'

He did not say anything; he seemed to be shrinking. You appeared at his side.

'What's wrong with, Mammy?'

He sighed: 'She's tired.'

'Can I help you, Pa?'

'I've done with work today. Shall we go to swim with the river-that-runs-both-ways instead?'

'You're not well, Jack. Please stay home. You need to rest.'

'Go and find your swim-suit and straw hat, Bel.'

The sound of snapping as he rubbed his grimy stalks together.

'Why are you not listening to me?'

'Hurry up, Sweet pea.'

'Jack!'

'Things will get better.'

I took his hand in mine. 'I hope so.'

I stood at the end of the wild garden and closed my eyes. Taking a deep breath, I imagined shift-shaping: a swallow, a salmon, a stag, a hare, a hawk, a butterfly, the vixen.

When I opened my eyes, I froze, despite the heat. Was that Mother foraging? She wore a long, black woolen coat and boots: strange garments to wear on such a hot day. My bottom jaw dropped. I tried to call, but no sound came out and my legs wouldn't move. So, I watched her.

Firstly, she gathered plants from the hedgerows. You see, Mother knew the ways of wild medicine. She could heal with roots and shoots. Next, she collected sheep's wool from brambles, picking out the burrs with her long, ringed fingers. I knew what she would do later. Wash it in the deep, stone sink and dye it in the dolly tub with plants from Back Field. Then she would spin the yarn on her wheel and knit hats and scarves and jumpers to keep me warm through the long winter which was cold and dark from November to February back then.

'Mother is in the trees of the wood,' I once said to you as we sat beneath an ash tree, whittling wands from its twigs. 'She jumps from the trees, to the hare, into me, from me, into you.'

You giggled when I told you that. 'I can see her, Mammy.'

We both could, couldn't we? We had other senses. There were other things we knew. Like Mother, we had the gift of second sight. I looked once more towards Back Field. But Mother was not there. Jack said I conjured her up from air. But I didn't.

You appeared at the back door. 'Ready Pa.'

Straw hat on your head, cute as a button. 'I can only swim backwards,' you said.

'Take care, Jack.'

'We will, won't we, Sweet pea?'

You nodded.

'Say good bye to Mammy.'

You ran over and hugged me. You were such a

sweetheart. I loved the bones of you. Still do.
Where are you?

ACORNS

We were sitting at the kitchen table. Jack not
meeting my eye. He was stirring slim branches
in the deep-blue sky. I guess he knew what I
was going to say.

'Have you seen a swallow yet?'

He stared at me and the sound was silence.

'I'm so worried, Jack.'

He put a leaf over my hand and shook his head.
Acorns fell onto the table.

'What can we do?'

'Nothing, but wait.'

I jumped up and sat down again, remembering
the ones we had buried under leaf litter. You
stopped eating oatmeal from the dish with
rabbits chasing each other round the rim and
stared at me, bottom lip quivering. I felt the
planet spinning faster. He smoothed your hair,
gave you a soft woody smile, handing you a piece
of bread. You shook your head.

'I'm not hungry anymore, Pa.'

I sighed, pushed my plate away.

'You've barely eaten for days,' he said to me, flickering into a moment of shade, not enough for respite from the heat.

'But the swallows should be here by now, Jack'

'Try not to get upset.'

There was an explosion in my chest, red mist.

'I *am* upset!'

A small animal whimpering. Arms round Jack's neck, your face buried in his nest. It was as if you grew from the same root. Moss had gathered in the creases of his knees. Were those grubs in his ears or honeybees? He sneezed and sneezed. Eggs pupating and hatching. He rocked out of balance.

'Don't cry, Sweet pea.'

You were hiccupping as you turned to me. 'I don't like it when Mammy's cross.'

A wall of ivy between us. The silence grew black with bacteria.

'You're distressing Bel.'

'I'm sorry.' And I was. But I was upset and angry too. I was losing my grip again. I just knew. But there was nothing I could do. 'Everything's going wrong,' I said, starting to weep.

He rustled and sighed not knowing what to say.

You both disappeared for a couple of days after that. I had no idea where you had gone. The bottom fell out of my world. I put my skirt on back to front and my shirt inside out. My arms and legs ached. All I did was shout. One night I felt a pain as if my ribs were popping and snapping, piercing my skin. I sat up in bed, sweat trickling down my chin. I cannot remember anything else.

When you returned Jack said you had been to the Seven Oaks Wood and asked me if I was feeling any better. I wasn't, but I told him I was. He didn't tell me workmen arrived and felled lots of trees. I found out later when he mumbled in

his dreams. My mind was a hive of bees.
History was repeating itself.

From then on, I got up earlier and earlier each
morning. Until I was rising in the middle of the
night, but I didn't see a single swallow or the
wild swan.

OAK TREE

The oak tree only had a couple of leaves on its branches that fourth spring. And there was a scar in the bark where there had been bacterial bleeding.

'Trees get poorly same as humans, Mammy.'

'I agree, Sweet pea. We must look after our beloved oak tree, mustn't we?'

You smiled at me. 'It's a special place for us and the fungi.'

'The insects and birds.'

'Bats and bees. Did you know, Mammy, it's home to the faeries.'

I nodded.

'And it's sacred to the goddess Ceres.'

I ruffled your hair. 'Bless you.'

For the first time since we had lived at our small, stone cottage, long-tailed tits did not build their ball nest in the fork of its trunk.

'Sometimes there are as many as two thousand feathers in a long-tailed tit's nest.' I once told Jack.

'Have you counted them?' he asked.

We laughed. We laughed lots in the old days. We were so happy. At least I thought we were, maybe I was wrong all the time?

Every day I climbed the oak tree, aware it was not there just for me, it had rights of its own and stood firm, knowing its place in the world. Tuning into its frequency, understanding its energy, I listened to it speak in soft stirring leaves, a gentle breeze guiding me, giving me strength and courage. Navigating the trunk, using holes and hollows, balancing on the lowest bough, between shifting branches and leaf dazzle. My mind keenly green, hearing it whispering in shivery roots, sharing its secrets and stories: the crowning of kings and queens, a meeting place, a spot for ceremonies, religious rites and to mark boundaries. The higher I climbed there was no me, just webs of life, thoughts and consciousness.

A wood mouse built its nest chamber under the roots. I saw it during the day, even though it was nocturnal: sandy brown fur, protruding eyes, large ears, long tail. You saw it too, do you remember?

'See Ki,' Mammy,' you said.

I picked you up. You smelled of teddy bears and river water. I am not sure how old you were then? Five or six, maybe seven?

'Do you mean the wood mouse?'

'Ki runs on fast feet up the tree.'

'Isn't he, sweet?'

'Ki is a being of the earth.'

I nodded. 'Yes, Sweet pea, that's true.'

'Ki-chi, the energy that runs through all things.'

Do you remember saying that? You were planting words like seeds. Me, the mother, the writer, was learning a lost language from you, the daughter, the teacher. I had forgotten so much, you see, that day you brought back a memory of Mother and me.

At dusk Mother took me to the forest where she lit a fire.

'This is a powerful place.' She told me. 'Here we can connect with the Otherworld and the spirit of the land.' Then she turned and spoke to a rock with all the respect she spoke to me. 'May we sit on you for a while?'

And we did, waiting patiently listening to the silence. I became sleepy. And just before I fell into a doze, a vixen came close, she sniffed me. As we moved to sit beneath a yew tree, she lay with her head on Mother's knee. As I touched the tree, the tree touched me. And I watched a spider spinning her web as Mother said:

'Everything is connected.'

Just then, a robin flew down and perched on her head, singing a song of scarlet and brown. And she whistled to him in a musical duet of the same language. It was magical, as if we were living in a faery tale.

Later that same day, when I was pulling up rotten carrots from the vegetable patch, I caught a glimpse of broad wings in the oak tree. I gritted my teeth. My palms were sweating. I was shaking.

'One for sorrow,' I said to Jack.

The words crawled off his earwig tongue: 'That's just superstition.'

'No, it isn't.'

'Yes, it is.'

'How do you know?'

He stomped up the path, stripped off his leaves, all tangles and thickets, dumping dead wood and balls of mistletoe. A hail of black pellets bouncing off my head, faeces from oak leaf roller caterpillars.

That night I woke and retched. I sat up and hugged my belly. It was as if my organs were shifting positions. Bending double, clutching my chest. I struggled and hissed. Toes cracking, splitting. My neck pulled taut, twisted out of itself. Eyes writhing to the back of my head. Fingers elongated, dislocated. I crawled out of bed, body inside out, my skin shedding white feathers.

'Jack! Help me,' I cried, but my mouth was squeezing into a hardness I didn't recognize. I pecked my own arms and legs. Gagging, convulsing and pulsing into something huge, disemboweling, aborting myself. My mind exploding into something so immense it filled the room, like the moon, incandescent and glowing. I shuddered and passed my innards on the floor with a shake and a shudder. Dragging my skin-bag across the floor warping and buckling, towards the door. The next morning, I woke wondering if it had all been a nightmare.

FLEDGLINGS

Two days' later, I was collecting kindling near the lean-to when it happened.

'Jack!'

He came out of the shed, red gold turning to mould when I got close to him, then black, like something dug up from a peat bog. I shuddered.

'Look, over there,' I said, pointing towards Green Valley. 'Someone has been hacking at the hawthorn hedge!'

Jack squinted his morning rain eyes into the distance.

'It's the nesting season! Did you know about it?'

'Of course not,' he said.

He swayed towards the shed a snail trail behind him.

'Jack, talk to me.'

He raised his branches to the sky, 'Why?'

'We need to do something!'

'How can we?'

'What's got into you?'

'It's not me, it's you.'

'No, it's not.'

'Yes, it is.' Then he said it. 'You're on the edge.'

I threw all the kindling onto the ground. 'No, I'm not!'

'Yes, you are.'

And in that split second, I realized, nothing would ever be the same again.

I bolted down the garden, Jack shrieking branches and leaves in the breeze after me, as I squeezed through the gap in the hedge. Then stopped. I strained my ears listening. And I heard Mother's voice,

'By attending to the voices of the birds you're learning the language of belonging.'

A solitary caw of a crow.

Tears sliding down my face, I ran over the field, stumbling along the hawthorn hedge, heart pumping, breath roaring, dropping to my knees

peering underneath. I unraveled a scream of
myself.

The ground was littered with twigs, straw, a
mess of smashed eggs. Featherless fledglings,
lavender-veined skins, beaks cracked open at
strange angles. Scratching the earth with bare
hands, tearing nails, bruising fingers, flinging
pinches of soil into space. At their wake I make
the mistake of warbling.

That night, in my writing room, sitting at my
desk, with a pain in my chest, I tried to write a
story about fledglings, to bring them back to life.
But I could not. So, I ripped every page out of
my journal and tore them into pieces. What was
the point of writing stories? What was the point
of anything?

You dawdled into the room and sat on my knee,
your forget-me-not blue eyes looking up at me,
wide and staring. Skinny legs dangling, trying to

wipe my tears away with your star hands. You
smelled of milk and honey. My love for you was
soft and warm and deep, something I often
buried myself in, but I wanted to be on my own
to mourn the fledglings.

'Cuddle me, Mammy.'

I ushered you out of the door and turned the key
in the lock. You knocked and knocked:

'Let me in.'

'Not by the hair of my chinny chin chin!'

'I want to sit on your knee, Mammy.'

'Leave me alone! Go and find Pa!'

'I am so sad. Kin are dead.' I think you said. But
your words were muffled as I put my head in my
hands and sobbed.

Later, I heard Jack swell and creak in the
kitchen. But I could not make out what you were
saying. I waited until he put you to bed. Then I
spent an age arranging candles around my
writing room, before lighting one for each bird I
had buried. I watched shadow flames flickering

over the walls, smelt the whiff of wax. Then I
climbed down the wooden ladder and stole out of
the back door.

It was crow-black outside. The air heavy with
dead birds. The moon dropped pools of guano
into the garden and clawed clouds around itself.
I looked towards the oak tree. Suddenly a
memory came back to me.

The first year we lived at the small, stone
cottage, a fledgling blackbird fell from his nest. I
picked it up and held it in my palm. It was both
soft and bony at the same time. Its heart beating
so hard, I could almost hear it, beak opening and
closing, looking at me with big eyes. I stroked its
breast with my little finger and spoke to him
gently.
'Don't be frightened.'

Jack carved a wooden box out of himself and I
filled it with dry grass. For over a week, you and

I took it in turns feeding the fledgling blackbird on insects, do you remember? Then, when it was strong enough, we took it to Back Field and set it free. I wished the hedge sparrow fledglings had been so lucky. I tried not to warble again thinking of their small, broken bodies, but my eyes went watery.

Part of me died that day.

The next morning Jack shouted rotting roots at me:

'What were you thinking? All those candles! We could have all been burnt alive!'

I never apologized. It embarrasses me now to think how reckless I'd been. I'm truly sorry, Bel. I hope you can find it in your heart to forgive me. You were only little and did not understand my moods. Neither did I, odd feelings just came over me, but that does not excuse my behaviour. I was wrong. I can see that now. I've no idea why I did not see it then. Maybe it was because all my energy was draining away, like Jack's.

Did I say that my memory is not all that it should be? There are lots of things I have forgotten. It was after that awful thing happened to Mother. I became unwell, have I said that already? It was such a trauma. I still haven't got my memory back. Not really. Perhaps I never will?

WILD SWAN

Jack spoke in the opening and closing of leaves.
'A few days away will take your mind off things.'
So, we drove to the coast, but it didn't. I fidgeted
all night keeping you and Jack awake. Even the
sound of the waves rushing to the shore didn't
soothe me. I was hot then cold, itchy and twitchy.

The next morning, we returned to our small,
stone cottage. When we got back, I ran to the
lake to look for the wild swan, but it wasn't
there. So, I hurried home to tell Jack. His
breath was a gale gone stale. 'You're just going
to have to accept it's gone.'
'But where?'
'I don't know?'
'You don't care.'
'Yes, I do, but you must let it go.'
His flesh translucent green. I let out a scream.
'You're driving yourself insane again.'
I shut up then.

It was the first of May. The sky a vivid blue. I wound May Day ribbon round the oak tree. And even though it was over thirty degrees, I built the bonfire.

At sunset we lit it. Jack was feeling a little stronger that day. He strummed his branches, long low notes with his bow. Then slides and slurs and double stops with fast fingers. As you and I danced barefoot wearing long, white dresses with garlands of wildflowers on our heads, whirling and twirling, clapping our hands to the sky, then down to the earth.

But it was the last time you, Jack and I celebrated Beltane. Please, be patient, I will tell you why later.

MAGPIE'S NEST

Are you wondering what Mother's story is? I
imagine you are. There are two parts to Mother's
story: the terrible and the enchanting. I'm not
sure you'll believe me when I tell you, but I
swear it's all true. Fact can be stranger than
fiction, can't it, Sweet pea? Are you too old to be
called Sweet pea now?

What I'm sharing with you are not facts; they are
shiny things. You see, my mind's a magpie's nest
that sparkles with trinkets. My pen is a faery
wand. I conjure magic from my imagination and
weave spells with my words. But you knew that,
didn't you? One day you said something that
took my breath away.
'Words make worlds, Mammy. They are
magical.'

JENNY WREN

Early morning, but as usual it was scorching. I
hadn't been able to sleep, not a peep. My body
was so hot, I thought it would set fire to our bed.

During the night Jack brought our mattress
downstairs and spread a cotton sheet over it. I
opened the doors to let fresh air in, but it was
soupy and stifling, so I let it out again.

Lying on top of the sheet, I watched the moon, a
silver ball, drift further and further away. And
strangely I slept. Yet, it was like swimming
under water and never coming up for air.

I was standing in Back Field near the oak tree,
scrunching my eyes in the sun to watch Jenny
Wren dart jerkily in the ivy on the front wall of
our small, stone cottage. Tiny tail cocked,
singing hugely, despite her small size. Had it
built a nest in there, I wondered? I crossed my

fingers. And toes.

Jack came out of the back door. 'Bel's still asleep.'

I nodded, not taking my eyes off Jenny Wren.

'I'm wilting in this heat.'

'Can I tell you something?'

'What?'

'Jenny Wren is the soul of the Oak.'

'I know.'

'And she's the queen of birds.'

He looked down. And frowned. A squirrel was scratching a hole in the ground.

'Is it?'

I nodded. 'The eagle and wren had a contest to see who could fly the highest. Unbeknown to the eagle, the wren rested on his back. As it grew tired, she lifted lightly and flew above him singing.'

I dared to look up at the sky then. Something I hadn't done for two days. But there were still no swallows. And I had no idea where the wild swan had gone.

BULLFINCHES

I was standing under an apple tree, tasting the coo-coo soothing sound of wood pigeons. Until insect wings of anxiety flickered in my throat and down to my belly as it came to my attention, I had not seen any blossom on its branches this year. A blade of distress sliced slowly beneath my ribs. No blossom meant no food for the bullfinches.

By the time Jack arrived home, my nerves were jangling. You were crying.
'I haven't been able to settle to anything today.'
'Can't you think of someone else for once in your life?'
'Watch out or I'll cut off your tail with a carving knife.'
He stared at me with leaves of dread as if I had grown another head. Balancing you on one bough, his forehead budding buds, he opened the cupboard door:

'Bread and cheese, Bel?'

You nodded.

'Have you seen any blossom on the fruit trees this year, Jack?'

He turned his back, hacked at the bread. You were on the chair beside him, chewing a crust.

I went to our carved, wooden bed. Even though it was suffocating, I pulled the eiderdown over my head and tasted dread. I could barely breathe and was soaked in sweat. I didn't care. When you came to say good-night, I feigned sleep. The next day, Jack said, that was mean and selfish of me. You were upset and had wet the bed.

'I'm so sorry,' I said.

LITTLE OWL

'Come with us, Mammy.'

I shook my head. You and Jack were going to swim with the river-that-runs-both-ways. But I was thinking of the swallows and wild swan, dead fledglings and spineless hedgehogs.

'What's happening, Jack?' I said.

Anxious suckers sprouted on his trunk as he ushered you out of the door.

I spent all morning polishing memories of our first three years at our small, stone cottage: clumps of primroses sparkling with dew, hares boxing, butterflies alighting on thistles, swallows migrating, hedgehogs hibernating. Before I realized where the time had gone, you were home with Jack, your hair dripping wet down your back.

'Why aren't you dressed?

I shrugged, my shoulders boulder-heavy. These days he had a knack of annoying me.

'Go and play, Bel. I want to talk to Mammy. No earwigging.'

But he didn't say a word to me or maybe I didn't listen? After that, I took to carrying books in my pocket, folklore and fairy tales. They comforted me, same as shift shaping.

I was sitting in the wild garden, the sun climbing high, when Jack asked me what I was reading. I didn't reply. I looked up at the sky. Not a single cloud in sight, but it was winter in me. And Jack still had a cough. His hands were clenched into fists of dead leaves. Not a single bud in sight. 'What's wrong?' he asked, gnawing on kernels. 'Nothing. I'm fine.'

But I wasn't, my moods were all over the place. Clenching my teeth, biting my lip, lifting my chin, I gave him a big grin, but he'd turned away, toppled towards the door, fell to the floor. What was wrong with him?

One night, when the blood moon rose, I heard a

howling. I shot up in bed. Jack beside me said:
'Talk to me.'

But he was hollowed out and I hadn't the energy
to explain. I didn't know how to explain. He
wouldn't have believed me anyway.

'I must have been dreaming. I'm sorry I woke
you.'

He gave my shoulder a squeeze, then went to
check on you, trailing spiders' webs and dead
flies. There I was again telling lies. I heard your
little voice:

'Sorry, Pa.'

There was the patter of feet and the flapping of
sheets. When he climbed back in bed, I
pretended to be asleep. He was soon snoring.
While I lay awake shaking like a leaf. Listening
to wolves howling, pages rustling. Until dawn
sieved black to blue, the start of a new day.

Sitting at the wooden table, eating bread and
honey. Jack was outside hanging out the clothes,
when down flew a blackbird and began to sing.

My heart lifted in my chest. But just then the chimney coughed and choked. Jack hadn't swept it. He usually did with good cheer, but not that year.

A little owl and a fall of sooty ash rolled onto the rug, startling himself as much as he startled me. It was grey, lying there, its big eyes bright with fright.

I opened the window and scuttled out of the room, hid in the kitchen, behind the large, wooden cupboard. Did an owl falling down a chimney signify change? I was not sure. I peeped round the door. I knew it was not going to be a change for the better, when I heard him, flying into the stone walls.

WOLF

Jack climbed down the wooden ladder as the clock struck midnight. I realize now he was in shock to see me golden-haired, hunched over a pile of books, wearing a long, silver gown, a garland of blossom on my head. The candle on the table at my side guttering and spluttering, dripping hot wax.

He flickered from the door across the floor. Swaying in the glow of the firelight for a very long time, as the rot set in.
'Why are you wearing a wig?'
'Why not?'
'And where did you get that dress?'
'Mother's dressing-up box.' There I'd said it. I didn't care anymore if he thought I was making things up. I was past caring. Everything was too much.
'What?'

'You heard me.'

I tried to keep the annoyance out of my voice. I wanted him to go away and leave me in peace. I was at a good bit in the story, where the woman was taking off her bodice, dress, petticoat, long wool stockings and throwing them into the fire. His speech was a storm brewing. 'I didn't know you had your Mother's dressing up box.' Wind rising and whistling. Black clouds fell from his mouth.

'There are lots of things you don't know about me.'

The branches of his hair shot through with terrible whips: 'There never used to be.'

'Everything changes, remember? You told me that, Jack.' I stood up, pushed him in the back. Books tumbling to the floor, waving my arms about. 'The hedges, trees, fields are changing. I don't know why. Do you? Are you involved in this conspiracy to destroy planet Earth too?'

He reformed into a towering version of himself.

His frown was thunder. His song sweeping the air lashing up fury. A terrible sound 'You're losing yourself in those books.' A shrieking. A howling.

'I'm losing lots of things,' I said, picking them up from the floor.

'Like being in touch with reality.'

I burst out laughing at that. When I could get my breath, I said: 'Reality is only a perception.'

'It's gone midnight.'

'Are you scared I'll turn into a pumpkin?'

I chuckled, but he did not join in. Was I getting under his skin? I did not know for sure. I did not know anything anymore. It was as if I was dreaming and wanting to wake up to discover I was dreaming.

Jack tried to whip the book from me, but I was too quick for him and leapt on the chair.

'This needs to stop!'

'Or what? Are you making threats?'

'You know, I'm not. Let's go to bed.'

'I'll come to bed when I like.'

He offered a foothold, thinking he was going to outwit me. But I knew every trick in the book. My guard was up. Crouching down next to me, pretending not to notice that my nails were bitten to the quick, but I liked my new habit, it went with my new look. Metamorphosis is the key to faery tales, Mother told me.

'What's wrong?' he whispered the storm passing over. 'Let's talk about this.'

I didn't reply; I don't know why.

'May,' he said tentatively, trying to take my hand, but I snatched it away. 'You're becoming paranoid.'

'No, I'm not!'

 But I was.

I stared over his shoulder, suddenly preoccupied. The moon was spilling milky pools through the

window. A wolf was howling. I did not say
anything though. Jack had a habit of accusing
me of imagining things. He said that the books
were to blame. They were taking over my life.
'On your way out, close the door.'
But he did not leave. He grounded himself. I
counted to ten.
'Ten green bottles standing on the wall. And if
one green bottle should accidently fall.'
'Stop singing.'
'I'm not singing.'
'Yes, you are.'
He left the room then, shutting the door softly
behind him like a secret.

Maybe I'm exaggerating, but I don't think so. I
know I have a vivid imagination. How could I
create stories otherwise? And I admit my
memories are vague, but I know I saw the wolf
through the window. He was prowling round the
garden, grey pelt bristling, orange eyes burning.

Was it coming with a warning?

I curled into a ball and rolled away from myself.

THE WATER PUMP

My gaze roamed the wild garden, loitering
behind the shed. All the plants were wilting and
dying. I remembered what Mother once said
when I was a small girl:
'If you care for the natural world, the natural
world will care for you too.'
You see, Mother wielded magic when her hands
connected with the earth. She coaxed life from
soil, nurtured tender shoots. She embraced
bulbs growing in the dark, developing the art of
deep listening.

I grabbed the buckets from where they were
leaning against the whitewashed wall in the
kitchen.
'Where are you going?'
'To fetch a pail of water.'
I worked the pump until sweat beaded my upper
lip and my arms dropped off. But there was not
a rush of water, simply a brownish trickle, relics

101

of leaves and seeds. There was a dull ache in my
head.

'I'm going back to bed. To mend my head.'

Would you like me to bring you anything?'

'Vinegar and brown paper.'

Then Jack fell down. And broke his crown. And
I came tumbling after.

ERA OF GREED

The heat had been pressing down for weeks and weeks, sucking the life out of everything. I was restless. Maybe a walk would clear my head? I'd barely stirred from our small, stone cottage in days, too tired after sleepless nights. Although the previous night I slept like the dead without dreaming.

Walking where the stream had once burbled and gurgled. The robin landed on the cracked ground, making a *tut-tut-tut* sound, flashing its red chest. Cocking its head on one side, glaring at me with black, beady eyes: *tut-tut-tut.* It flew onto my head, then onto my shoulder: *tut-tut-tut.* 'What are you trying to tell me?' I stroked its head with my little finger. 'What is it?'

And then I saw it, nailed to the trunk of a beech tree: **LAND SOLD: A HUNDRED ACRES OF DEVELOPMENT OPPORTUNITIES**

Momentarily I was stunned like someone who
had been blinded by the afterglow of a spark
from a bonfire and was waiting for sight to come
back.

I ran all the way back to our small, stone cottage.
Robin flying just in front of me, *tut-tut-tut.*

Crashing through the door, crying, gasping,
choking, like a character in the wrong story.
Jack put the kettle on. I took it off again.
'Have you seen the sign?'
Hairy nettles grew between his toes and out of
his nose: 'We both knew something like this was
going to happen!'
His words stung me. 'That's true.'
And it was. I had had this strange feeling since
the magpie's warning.
You climbed the wooden ladder to your bedroom.
'Now, look what you've done. Branches rattling
like antlers. 'Why do you always let your
emotions spill all over the place?'

I sat down then because my legs were shaking. He went to hold me, but I pulled away.

'Fee fie fo fum,' I said in a low, deep voice. 'I smell the blood of an English man. Be he alive or be he dead.' I grabbed the twigs of his shirt. 'I'll grind his bones to make my bread.' Then I shoved him backwards. He fell over, cracking his crown on the hat and coat stand. His eyes rolled back in their hollows. I think you came downstairs then. I can't remember, but I do remember shouting at him.

'Don't ever touch me again without permission.' My scarf slipped over my eyes. Golden hair streamed down my face. You were screaming and crying.

'Stop it, Mammy!'

And I was shouting: 'I can't bear to be touched. If you touch me, I'll fall apart. And all the king's horses and all the king's men will never put me back together again.'

'Mammy! I don't like it.'

Jack staggered to his roots, leaves falling into his

eyes. 'What's wrong with you?'

'There's nothing wrong with me.'

'You just said you're falling apart!'

'I said if you touch me again...'

'You're being bizarre.'

'No, I'm not.'

'Yes, you are.'

'You're a poet.'

'You're crazy.'

'No, I'm not.'

'Yes, you are!'

'You're speaking a language of loss. Look at you, all covered in moss.'

I realize now I was acting strange. But who could blame me? The planet was spiraling out of control, but Jack said it was me that was spiraling out of control. Maybe I was, but the planet was too, caused by the people living there.

I didn't sleep that night. Jack did. He lay beside me snoring. I got up at three in the morning to look for the wild swan, but she was not at the lake. So, I sat in the wild garden waiting for the swallows, but they did not arrive.

BOG FIELD

The next morning, we were distant and cold with each other as we ate our breakfast. Jack, twisting his tendrils, watched my every move. 'I spy with my little eye,' I said to Jack, pushing my bowl of oatmeal across the table. They spied on me. And now he was spying on me. Just like when I was in that hell hole, did I ever tell you about that? It was before I met Jack, not long after Mother disappeared. There, I've said it, Mother disappeared. One day she went foraging and never returned. Unbelievable how someone can disappear just like that. Here one minute, gone the next. Did I ever mention that terrible time to you? Did Jack?

It was late afternoon and Mother still was not home. So, I decided to go and look for her. I kept to the path for a while, then, took a short cut to the village past Bog Field. Someone was calling to me.

And then I saw her, Mother, up to her neck in mucky gloop, struggling in the slimy wetness. Mouth coffin-wide screaming my name; or was it me screaming her name? Had she slipped from the path? Had someone pushed her? There were rumours in the village. Some said Mother was a witch, others that she was a visitor from the spirit world. Menfolk gossiping about her. They were jealous of her wisdom and magical powers of healing.

Her squeal was that of slaughtered pig as, before my eyes, she was sucked under. The blood drained from my body. I was standing in a puddle of it, warm and wet, lapping my ankles. Did I run to the village for help? I don't remember. All I recall is waking up in that hell hole. I've no idea how I got there. I imagine you're thinking: She's made it all up. After all, she is a storyteller. But it is true, every single word of what I've just told you.

Memories of life with Mother only started coming back to me after I'd given birth to you.

Jack was with me, during labour, rubbing my back, mopping my brow as red-hot pokers of pain ripped across my belly. I grunted and growled, an animal, on all fours, bearing down, head thrust back, baying and howling. Until you tore into the world, mewling. Tiny limbs moving in slow motion. Joy exploded in my solar plexus as I drowned in your forget-me-not-blue eyes.

I don't remember the first year of your life. It was as if I'd fallen down a long, dark tunnel and couldn't find my way out. And so, I was taken into that hell hole. Again.

I only recovered when we moved to our small, stone cottage. I was so happy living there. I wrote lots of stories before the magpie's warning, after that, I wrote nothing, not until Mother

came back.   Yes, that's right, Mother came back.
I'll tell you about that some other time.

DAISY FIELD

Do you remember the wildfire in Daisy Field?
The workmen told me not to worry. They would
put it out. I didn't believe them.
'All the animals will be burnt alive!' I cried.
'Go back home. Everything will be alright!'
They lied.

Before the era of greed, we spent hours making
daisy chains in Daisy Field, do you remember?
Fastening them round our neck and wrists,
placing them like tiaras on our heads.
'Each tiny flower tells a story,' I said.
And now every single one of them, like the
animals were dead.

We did not celebrate the summer solstice. Just
as I was going to bed you said something strange:
'They can't hide the fires anymore, Mammy.'

BACK FIELD

The sun pounded down on me as I walked
through Back Field. Suddenly I had a curious
sense of being watched.   I dropped to my knees
rolled over in the parched grass, yelling:
'Show yourselves!'
But no one did. There was only the robin flitting
through the hedges like a spark from a fiddle.

When we had first moved to the small, stone
cottage, there had been swarms of bright orange
and brown insects fizzing over nettles and
thistles. Trips of rabbits lolloped through long
grass and red admiral butterflies settled on
wildflowers. Not anymore. Nothing grew there.
There had been the screeches of dusky-pink jays
as they crashed through ash trees. And the
musical notes trilling and cascading like gold
coins as skylarks flew up from the earth to the
sky. I had not heard their song in a long time.
Or seen the stoats dancing down prey, leaping

and thrashing, spinning and jumping,
performing back flips, hypnotizing crow chicks,
creeping nearer and nearer and nearer, until
delivering the kill. Will things ever be the same
again?

I felt a bit funny and couldn't stop laughing. Yet,
there was nothing to laugh about. My world had
fallen apart. Terror gnawed away at me. I
wanted to fly out of my body into the air where
buzzards once circled and red kites rode
thermals.

We'd been living the faery tale. Yet, I realized
that not all faery tales have happy endings
because that day there weren't any insects or
skylarks, sheep or buzzards, red kites or jays,
stoats or rabbits and not a single red admiral
butterfly. There was a solitary black and white
cow. I stopped in my tracks and said:
'I must take the cow to market and sell her,
before she jumps over the moon.'

'Not everything's **FOR SALE** around here,'
mooed the cow, gawping at me with big, brown
eyes, ears twitching. Its tail flicking flies away.
A soft fall of muck and moo. And I felt a flame of
shame: What had I been thinking?

I'd once seen a cow lying on its side in Back
Field. I thought it was dead but as I approached
its leg jerked. And then I saw the hooves of a
calf coming out of its body.

A flare of panic but excitement too. Within
seconds, I crouched in the grass, sleeves rolled
up, my arm inside the cow. It felt warm and
weird like a huge, sloppy mouth sucking
ferociously on my arm. I did not like it and
neither did the cow. It mooed and groaned. But
I wanted to help. I was tugging and tugging
until a massive bellow and the calf rushed out
with a gush and whoosh of fluid. Are you the
cow that gave birth that day, I wondered?

Just then the wise-woman appeared. She wore
an olive-green dress and big boots. Her face was
wrinkled as a pickled walnut.

'The small, stone cottage belongs to you,' she
said. 'But a wicked giant will steal it.'

I knew what she said was true. And there was
nothing I could do about it.

I continued walking, hoping to see the vixen,
grooming her rust-red pelt, one amber eye on her
cubs chasing each other, bounding and leaping,
play fighting, learning survival skills. The dog
fox, slim and long with pointy ears, watching on.
Spooning in bed with Jack we often heard the
high-pitched, blood-curdling screams of the
vixen's 'love song', the one she made during sex.
We had not heard it that year. And we had not
been spooning.

'The dish ran away with the spoon,' I said to Jack
one night in bed.

He did not reply. At the time, I did not know

why. I do now: how can you have a conversation with a crazy woman?

And then I saw it, robin impaled on one of the thorns of the blackthorn tree, the butcher bird's larder. My blood ran cold.
'Who killed cock robin?' I yelled. 'Was it you, sparrow?'
'Yes, with my bow and arrow!'
'I saw him die,' said the fly, buzzing around my head.
'Go away,' I said, tears running down my cheeks.
'With my little eye, I saw him die,' said the fly.
'Who'll make his shroud?'
'I,' said the beetle glistening on a thorn. 'With my needle and thread.'
But just then robin opened his beak and sang. I put my hand to my head and spun round and round stumbling over a decapitated woodpigeon: a sparrowhawk's kill?

Once, when I'd been in the wild garden, a sparrowhawk plummeted from the sky like a shooting star, seized a blackbird from where he was singing on the lean-to and took off in a blaze of ferocious energy with it held fast between its talons.

Suddenly, I heard low voices. A pack of workmen wearing florescent orange jackets and hard, white hats strode past, at first, they did not see me. I hid behind the oak tree, it protected me, but then, when I was walking towards the hedge, I heard a gruff voice shout:

'What do you think you're doing?' A workman was gesticulating wildly, red in the face, glaring at me. 'This is private land!'

'The land belongs to itself.' I muttered under my breath as I turned to walk back to our small, stone cottage.

BATS

Early evening, the sun fell behind the stone wall,
leaving an egg yolk dribble in the sky as I
wandered over Back Field filling my basket with
twigs. Wondering why there were burn scars,
soot and ash.
'Surely you're not going to light a fire in this
heat?' Jack swayed into deadly nightshade at
the bottom of the wild garden. I didn't tell him
why I was doing it or even answer him. I had a
plan.

A hot breeze whispered sweet nothings to me
through the leaves of the oak tree, but then,
without warning there was a change to gale force
and a stifling wind whined and screamed:
'I'll huff and I'll puff and I'll blow your house in!'
'Not by the hair of my chinny chin chin. You'll
never blow our small, stone cottage in!'

After chopping logs in the shed, I made the fire
in the living room, putting sticks on kindling
which caught fire quickly, burning and crackling.
Soon a pyramid of logs glowed as I placed a
cauldron of water to boil. Then I took it off
again.

For hours I sat by the fire warming my pretty
toes, imagining the charcoal line drawn from our
small, stone cottage chimney to the treetops. I
thought I heard him prowling around on the roof.
Goblins of fear scrambling to get out of me.

Jack laid down in rings on the living room floor,
roots torn up, telling me the talk of the village:
extreme heatwaves, storms, flash floods,
wildfires. Then he burst into a filigree of dust,
smelling of must.

You were sleeping upstairs.

I crept into the kitchen and opened the large, wooden cupboard to get the tea caddy, but slammed it shut again when I saw meat and a bottle of blood on the shelf. I did not recall putting them there. Had one of those workmen sneaked into our small, stone cottage and done it? Just then a black cat appeared and said: 'A slut is she who eats the flesh and drinks the blood of her granny.'

Then it shivered to fur and bones and vanished.

It was so hot I stripped to my underwear and fell asleep in the rocking chair. When I woke, I plotted how to kill the men with wolf-grins. A swift blow with the axe, slice open their bellies and fill them with large stones. So, when they tried to run away, the stones were so heavy they dropped down dead. I found that funny. I was laughing as I imagined skinning their bodies and making coats. Just then, Jack appeared in a crush of leaves, rocking unsteadily: dark spots on his trunk:

'A fungal sickness of tiredness,' he said.
But I was not really listening. I told him about
the meat and blood and black cat. Without
saying anymore, he notched towards the door, a
wisp of breeze blowing through him, leaving me
alone again.

I dampened down the embers and sat among the
cinders, waiting for him to return, going
outside every five minutes to see where he was.

There were humps of bushes and silhouettes of
trees in the wild garden. The moon was clear
and bright. A greater horseshoe bat darted from
dim mauve shadows under the eaves of our
small, stone cottage. Flapping and fluttering,
flying in chattering circles above my head, so
close, its wings touched my hair. Diving and
swooping heading for the fruit trees to pick
dorbeetles and moths from the leaves, but they
were sparse, same as the blossom, same as the
bats, butterflies, rabbits, hares, cuckoos. And

the swallows.

I went inside and climbed the wooden ladder,
saying:
'Here comes a candle to light you to bed. And
here comes a chopper to chop off your head.'
I stumbled on the top stair. 'Ssh,' one finger on
my lips, giggling. 'Be quiet,' I stuttered and
spluttered falling against your bedroom door. So,
I looked in. I had not been drinking sloe gin.
Perhaps just a little. Mother's ruin. Jack said I
drank too much. I needed to see a doctor. And I
laughed in his face, shouting:
'DOCTOR FOSTER'S GONE TO
GLOUCESTER!'

Moonlight lit up your tiny room which smelt of
dust and timbers. Your straw-hat dangled from a
big wooden peg through a beam. It had a pale
blue ribbon round its brim. Your rabbit slippers,
long ears and bob tails on the heels were by the
door, waiting for you to step into them. There

was a small chest of drawers. You kept your box
of treasures under the bed: marbles, tree sap,
pebbles, bangles, beads and shells.

You were asleep in the bed looking lost. As if you
were sleeping in Daddy Bear's bed. Your dreams
drifting round the room soft as moths settling on
your face. I caressed your soft, peachy cheek,
stroked you under the, chinny chin chin.
'Sugar and spice and everything nice,' I said,
bending at the waist to kiss your forehead. You
tasted of faery stories and buttercups.

In our bedroom, I lit a candle; immediately the
room was given back its furniture. There was
our carved, wooden bed and an old mattress
propped against one wall, a dressing table and a
dusky-pink and turquoise rag rug on the floor.
That was all. The ceiling was so sloped at each
end of the room, I had to stoop to lift the latch on
the small window.

The moon smiled at me as the wind lifted my hair gently breathing hot breath on my neck.

The trees were tangled with words and stars.

I stretched my hand against the wall and our small, stone cottage warmed my palm like an old friend.

Once, when we had been to a festival in the village, we arrived home at midnight. I got out of the truck and gazed around me. I pushed the gate open. It flattened the grass, pushing back nettles and brambles and dandelion clocks. Our small, stone cottage was sleeping, just waiting for me to bring it back to life. I ran my hands over its walls, still mellow from the day's sunshine.

'I've missed you,' whispered our small, stone cottage.

'I've missed you too. I'm so glad to be back.'

I was not crazy then, was I?

I went to bed straining to hear mice scurrying in the loft. They appeared during the spring, eating everything, not this year.

Where was Jack?

Was that him tapping at the windows, crying through the lock?
'You're sure of a big surprise,' I said, slipping out of my underwear, running naked downstairs, letting him in.
'If you go down in the woods,' he replied. 'You'd better go in disguise.'
'Not by the hair of my chinny chin chin.'
And we laughed and laughed and laughed until our small, stone cottage fell in. But none of this really happened. I was imagining things. Again.

I fell into a restless doze, dreaming of burnt land,

dead fledglings and a pack of workmen wearing florescent orange jackets and hard, white hats. And I was stalking them, brandishing an axe.

'I don't feel very well this morning,' I said, when I woke. 'My head is throbbing.'
'Stay in bed. I'm going for the doctor,' said Jack, pulling on crisscross shadows of sunlight, heady with odours of green, stubbing out a solitary bud. His back splattered with mud.
'I don't need the doctor. I'm just tired. Leave me alone,' I said.
I heard your voice then:
'Pa, I'm hungry. Can I have my breakfast.'
'Go and see to Bel,' I said.

For six days and six nights I did not get out of bed.

But you will never believe what happened on the seventh day.

ARABESQUES OF HOPE

I woke on the seventh day with a light feeling in
my belly like spring had arrived overnight, and it
had!   When I opened the bedroom window a
crack there was a bright flash. Exploding over
the roof of our small, stone cottage in spangles of
sunlight, showing their royal-blue backs and
scarlet throats.   Arabesques of hope. I called out
to Jack. Forgetting you and he were away,
leaving me alone.

Without dressing I ran downstairs and into the
wild garden. A skim of swallows overhead,
circling the shed.
'Welcome home! Welcome home!'

I watched them all day. The weathervane
creaking in a sulky breeze. I was still watching
them, when you and Jack returned, shadowy as
ghosts in the half-light. I told him about the

swallows as he lifted you out of the truck. You were sleeping against his solid wood as he carried you inside, helped you undress, tucking you in bed, kissing your dandelion head.   And he didn't say one word to me.

Taking a cotton sheet from the cupboard, I opened the back door.
'I'm going to sleep outside so I can see the swallows at first light.' Then I shut the door behind me.
'Good night.'

MOLES

The heat hung around our small, stone cottage throwing its weight about like a bully. I wiped sweat from my brow. My shirt was sticking to my back. You were outside with Jack sitting on Mother's quilted blanket wearing a lovely cotton dress of rainbow colours.

I kept the blade of the scythe flat and low, swinging it in an arc, a slow, steady rhythm, listening to the soothing silky sound of the slashed grass whispering to the ground, releasing its sweet scent. Gathering it up, placing it on our wheelbarrow, which I pushed to the bottom of the wild garden towards the compost-heap. This was where the earth worms and slugs and snails once lived. The dome of sandy soil which once stirred with ants, nest building, digging tunnels, gathering food, had gone.

The words blackened my mouth and scalded my tongue: '**LAND SOLD: A HUNDRED ACRES OF DEVELOPMENT OPPORTUNITIES**.'

'What did you say?' asked Jack, the dark bud dead in his eyes.

I looked to the skies: 'Nothing.'

'Let me scythe. You rake the grass.'

'Yes, sir,' I replied, dropping him a curtsey.

'Three bags full.'

A blackbird followed me round the garden hoping for a feast of fat, juicy earthworms.

'There aren't any,' I said. 'Can't you see, the ground is baked and cracked?'

And all the while Jack watched me. Maybe he is worrying about something, I thought. Now I realize that he was worrying about me, but I was elsewhere. I wish things had turned out differently.

I went for a walk, passing a sign at the side of

the road, next to a lone dandelion: **KEEP OUT CONSTRUCTION.** I felt hot then cold. Two long-tailed tits flitted between the branches of a dying ash tree, tumbling and somersaulting, chivvying each other on. In the fields, there were dried-up mounds of earth, but no sign of any moles: black velvet fur, blind eyes, shovel feet, long, curved claws.

I took the footpath running behind the hedge, breaking into open land. There was another sign:
MAJOR WORKS TO START HERE SOON. If I moved, even a little bit, my head would flash bright; lightning strike smack into static. So, I stood very still indeed.

All the next day I tended my herb patch. And the day after. And the day after that. Herbs for anxiety: lemon balm and passionflower. I put dried lavender under my pillow to help me sleep at night, but it did not. And I piled mattresses on top of each other, but there was a hard lump in the bed. I told Jack I could feel the pea because I was a princess. I think there were tears in his eyes he was so happy he was married to royalty.

I was standing near the swing that Jack had tied to a branch of the oak tree, pulling down on it time after time, testing to see if it was safe for you. Now it was moving gently backwards and forwards in the wind, creaking softly, rocking like a cradle and I was singing:
'When the bough breaks, the cradle will fall. And down will come baby, cradle and all.'

DEVIL BIRD

In Back Field, ox-eye daisies once grew in
profusion, tall on slender stalks, milky-white
petals, gleaming yellow centres, but there were
only a few this year.

'At dusk, the ox-eye daisy does not close, it glows
like a fallen moon, I told you.

And you nodded. I pointed to a solitary foxglove.

'Elves and faeries place their fingers inside these
flowers.'

You nodded again, not saying anything. Pink
dog roses lolled over a hawthorn hedge. It was
August, usually they bloomed in June. Suddenly
you said:

'Mammy why aren't you writing stories
anymore?'

'I can't,' I said.

'That's sad, Mammy.'

'It's because I'm mad.'

'You are funny.'

'Funny as a bunny.'

'Eating honey.'

'Silly you.'

'I don't want to play this game anymore, Mammy. Pa says it's silly talking in rhyme.'

'I want to. There was an old woman who lived in a...

'I'm going to find Pa.'

'Shoe, she lived in a shoe! Come back when I'm talking to you!'

Do you remember us standing in shafts of sunlight by the stream watching the blood-red flash of sticklebacks? They darted through weeds, fins fluttering like tiny knives. We sang: 'One, two, three, four, five, once I caught a fish alive.'

There was a time when nettles flared like green flames and were covered in painted ladies, red admirals, meadow browns, swallow-tails and orange-tips, not anymore. And most of the thistles had died.

I sat in the middle of Back Field, the deepest sadness squatting between my lungs, it took so much effort to breathe.   I imagined I was a devil bird, shutting off half of my brain, eating, drinking and sleeping on the wing.

Things changed so much when the developers moved in, Sweet pea. We lost the land without leaving it, didn't we?

WORKMEN

Shuddering and crashing, thundering and
pounding. I lay there, listening in the dark,
sweating all over. Adrenalin rushing round my
body. My heart racing. It was as if a metal bolt
was being tightened in my chest. Still I lay
there. My hands over my ears, trying to shut out
the thump and drone of machinery. Suddenly I
couldn't bear it any longer. I got up, careful not
to disturb Jack. I crept past your door, down the
wooden ladder, a desperate rage running through
my veins. Slowly I opened the back door. There
was a hot reek of chemicals, a stink of smoke.
And the noise was deafening.

The full-fat, creamy-white moon was wreathed in
smog. I could not see the stars. The night
glowed orange as I stole along the path. I took
the axe from the shed. Holding it over one
shoulder, I squeezed through the gap in the
hawthorn hedge and trudged over Back Field

like a burglar from a children's storybook.

My torch floodlit the diggers and cranes and trucks, but they stood silent and still. Had I imagined the workmen toiling through the night?

I climbed into the back of a truck cradling the axe. I waited and waited. Eventually, I gave up and trudged home to our small, stone cottage, letting myself in through the back door.

With a heavy heart, I climbed the wooden ladder. And with great care, so as not to wake you and Jack, I hid the axe under the bed, slipping back under the cotton sheets next to him.

The next morning Jack startled me awake giving me a shake.
'What were you planning to do with this?' he asked, weighing the axe with both hands. The head gleaming in the sun blazing in through the bedroom window. His mouth tightened into a

knot of disapproval. Despite the heat, he was shivering. I didn't dare tell him that I was planning to behead the workmen one by one. The heat was breathless. I stared through the window. The sky was a pulsing, metallic blue.

'Oh, Jack, I don't know what I was thinking.'

He left the room then. I watched him from out of the window as he went into the shed with the axe and re-appeared without it. He locked the shed door. I dashed down the wooden ladder, raced out into the wild garden as Jack's truck pulled out onto the lane.

I do not remember leaving you at home alone while I went for a walk, but I must have done because when I returned, you had gone. I flew round our small, stone cottage, searching everywhere:

'Bel! Bel!'

But I could not find you anywhere. Outside, I raced down the path, screaming:

'Where are you?'

I crashed into the lean-to, pulling out logs, but you were not there. Inside the toilet shack, looking into the trees, peering over the hedge. I was sobbing and sobbing.

'Bel! Bel! Where are you?'

By early evening I was at my wits' end, sitting on the stone step, waiting for Jack. Yet, when he drove through the gates, you were sitting beside him in the truck.

SOLASTALGIA

Snapping and snarling, growling and howling,
saliva dripping from his jaws:
'Come, get into bed with me.'
'What a deep voice you have,' I said.
'All the better to greet you with, my dear.'
I swallowed my fear, backing towards the door:
'What a big mouth you have.'
'All the better to eat you with, my dear.
And he leapt from the bed, pinning me to the
floor, claws worrying at my throat.

I jack-knifed up in bed sweating and screaming.

I hid with the dust balls and goblins under the
bed. It took all morning for the doctor to
persuade me to crawl out, so, Jack said. The
doctor told me I was suffering from *solastalgia*. I
think that's what he said.

When the needle pierced my skin, I fell into a

deep pool of myself, the colour inside eyelids
when dreaming.

My limbs were soft and stretchy: syrupy sweet.
My head lolled onto my chest, eyes rolling back
in my head. I heard Jack and the doctor talking,
but I could not make out what they were saying.

Later, much later, I think I heard Jack's voice far
away:
'Mammy's tired. Let's leave her to sleep.'
'For a hundred years,' I said.

HUMMING-BIRD HAWK-MOTH

When I opened my eyes, I was alone in the wild
garden, dreamy and sleepy. I watched a
slowworm slither like quicksilver, coiling,
uncoiling, gliding into a clump of tall, dry grass,
melting away. Plums that could not bear their
own weight fell to the ground with gentle thuds.
The air hummed. I was nowhere and I was
everywhere, lolling in a wicker chair, as the late
afternoon folded into a peach and apricot
evening. And I wondered why I was still there
when night descended like a black, wool blanket,
a tree became a witch, a bush a dwarf, a flower a
faery. But there were no bats.

Was the vixen barking in Back Field? Was the
hare leaping over Seven Stars hills? Was the
barn owl screeching in the oak tree? I listened
hopefully, but nothing. I dropped like a stone
into the well of silence. And I just knew Jack
would say:

'Oh, May, you've been cloud walking again.'

Well, let him.

Tea-lights burning on the stone steps were once
magnets for moths: mottled beauty, white
ermine, heart and dart, ruby tiger, their wings
soft pastel against a sky the colour of charcoal.
My favourite was the humming-bird hawk-moth;
it hovered over the honeysuckle, feeding with its
long proboscis, wings beating so fast they
hummed but I had not seen one for ages. And I
hadn't seen any honeysuckle. And although we
slept with our windows open, we rarely found
tiger moths or crane-flies in our bedroom in the
morning anymore.

By the end of the week the landscape was
littered with piles of churned up earth. Stacks of
rubble. Bundles of barbed wire. There were
drain rods and clamps, diggers and ramps.
Sheets of corrugated iron. Portable cabins.
Pipes and diggers. Bags of rubbish which stank.

And signs:

**NO ACCESS FOR UNUNAUTHORISED
PERSONS**.

Jack didn't look well. His eyes were chlorophyll
bright. His hands balled tight. I think he was
struggling to keep himself together. Soon he
would be a pile of sawdust on the floor and I
would have to brush him up. I was shaking and
shaking and shaking. He dropped a small blue
pill into my cupped hand and I swallowed it with
a sip of water.

When I woke up, it was going dark. Tiny feelings
were creeping out of the shadows. There was an
ache in my chest for all the lost species.

Splinters of sadness pierced my skin. I tried to
smile when Jack took my hand, but I felt lost,
lost in the forest and I had forgotten to drop a
trail of tiny, white pebbles to show me the way
back to myself.

Holding each other, softly, silently Jack and I shuffled to bed like old people, sadness leaking through the small, stone cottage.

When we first moved into our small, stone cottage, lying in our bed at night, I had never known anything like the darkness in our bedroom. It was as if my eyes were still closed when they were open, it was so black, but now the bedroom glowed orange. Birds twittered all night. I had loved feeling safe and unreachable, deep in the countryside, but I knew now that feeling safe was just an illusion.

Time became stretched out of shape, full of holes, I fell through them into the next day, the next night, the next day, the next night and nothing felt right.

The ancient track was filled with the low rumble of lorries. Bottle tops, ring pulls, food wrappers, cans spilled from plastic bags.

Bulldozers were ramping in the Green Valley levelling a road. There was scaffolding and construction sheeting, cables, fencing. And more signs: **DANGER KEEP OUT**

It was the autumn equinox. Still no clouds in the pure, blue sky. I stood in the wild garden. The sun a branding iron slammed between my shoulder blades. The air hotter than a furnace; it was as if the whole country was burning its forests and grassland. I could not remember the sound of rain, the smell or feel of it on my skin. The earth was scorched and barren. I stared at the trees, their black branches twisted like crones.

I recalled the times we harvested the apples. Placing our cupped hands under each fruit, gently lifting and twisting. I loved the round, smooth feel of them in my palms. We put the damaged ones on the compost heap or left them where they fell for the birds. Others, we wiped

147

with a soft cloth and wrapped them in muslin as if they were fine bone-china, storing them in the wooden cupboard. They lasted us all through the long, winter months.

There were very few berries on the hawthorn hedges, no acorns on the oak tree and not enough rose hips to make syrup.

I felt so sad I wanted to burrow under the compost heap and gnaw on vegetable peelings with the maggots. Instead I swallowed a large, white pill and floated out to sea in a beautiful pea-green boat.

BADGER

I saw him in my dreams before I found him, in a heap at the side of a ditch, amongst empty cans sheets of plastic, rolls of barbed wire. From a distance he appeared unmarked, eyes closed, as if he was sleeping peacefully. Badger, who lived in the Wild Wood. But as I got closer, I saw it was dead, a lump of flesh and bones, fur and congealed blood.

Suddenly, I had a sudden vision of Mother lying deep in the bog. Skin stretched over her bones. Mouth frozen in a scream. I could taste her with my eyes, smell her with my teeth, see her with my ears. Mother was everywhere. She was the skein of wool that weaved through the blankets of fields, clouds and trees, birds, rivers, fish, animals, flowers and leaves. I thought of the times we had lit a fire in the hearth of the small, stone cottage: the logs smoking, burning, becoming ash, ash that we scattered over the

compost heap;
Ashes to ashes
Dust to dust.
'Nothing is lost,' Mother once told me.
'Everything just changes form.'

I crouched over the badger, taking in the lips
curled over his teeth. Gently, I stroked its
ghostly, grey pelt, touched his black and white
snout partially ensnared in a plastic bag blowing
in a hot breeze, its stumpy tail and legs. His
claws were like shovels for burrowing deep
underground to forage for earth worms and
slugs, although there had not been many of those
this year.

I wanted to bury the badger, return him to the
earth, but I hadn't got a spade with me. Besides,
the ground was rock hard from lack of rain. So,
I covered him with a few leaves, kicking away
the trash.

And I stayed until dusk fell lifting the scent of old bones.

STARLINGS

A lorry, a crane and a forklift truck were parked next to the oak tree. Workmen in florescent orange jackets and hard, white hats were shouting to each other in gruff voices. I dashed down the wild garden, freezing on the spot as I saw them putting on ear-protectors and gloves.

There were two of them holding the chainsaw.

A thrum, a mechanical whine, a growl.

I howled as it yowled, the noise drilling through my teeth.

Scream of splitting wood. Spit of sawdust.

Leaves rustling and shivering, sweating and quivering, sucking and excreting. The oak tree closing its crown. There was fear in its frown. A deep gash in its side.

Squirrels and mice bolted. A swarm of bees fell
like a curtain disappearing over Back Field. A
woodpecker tumbled from its nest. Butterflies
flittered through the air in a chaos of colours.
A murder of crows squawked and cawed flying off
in all directions.

Before it fell, the oak tree moaned and groaned.
A creaking. A shrieking. A deep-dark cracking.
The ground quaking and shaking as it tumbled
and fell with an almighty thud vibrating through
the planet.

The oak tree's root ball quivered like tentacles,
sap bleeding into the earth.

You were screaming and screaming and
screaming and screaming.

Jack was shouting and swearing and stuttering

and stumbling.

I was too shocked to do or say anything.

And. Then. For a moment. All was deathly quiet.

Until I heard him.

Jack weeping.

'Hundreds of years' growth ended in less than an hour,' he sobbed. Another life taken. An entire woodland community gone.'

And with that he fell to the ground without another sound.

The executioners whooped and patted each other on the back.

Suddenly there was a cacophony of shrieking and

twittering, the air swelling with sound, sonorous and soft all at the same time.

I looked up.

The sky was shivering and quivering, heaving and plunging, rippling and rolling, petrol-blue, emerald-
green, jet-black, coming to the boil like oily water then one dropped
Another
Another
And another
Fast and furious
It was raining starlings. I stood there, unable to speak, my open mouth full of feathers and tiny bones.

MORE SIGNS

Where I once stood to meditate in Back Field
with a view of Green Valley, where milk had
collected like clotted cream in a bowl, there was a
road. Further on, there were numbered districts
and housing estates named after the habitats the
developers had destroyed: *Primrose Walk,
Bluebell Close, Wild Wood Way.* Beyond there
was the forest.

A ragged buzzard with dull, dead eyes squatted
on a sign: **LUXURY CAR SHOWROOM
COMING SOON**.

Cardboard boxes cartwheeled across a grass
verge. Cans clattered along a kerb where the
stream had been.

There were sheets of polythene tangled in fences
and flapping in the hedges like banners. There

were empty bottles and a fallen willow tree.

There were vehicles being clamped.

There was a half-built pub and a hotel with a
sign: **LUNCH IN 15 MINUTES-THAT'S OUR
PROMISE.**

Near the health club and piles of rubbish there
was a small patch that had been reclaimed, a
designated conservation area, fenced off,
sanitized: bird boxes, rustic picnic tables, litter
bins, rules and regulations:

**KEEP TO THE PATHS
LOOK CAREFULLY TO SEE THE WILDLIFE
24 HOUR CCTV SURVEILLANCE**

For a month I never left our small, stone cottage.

EULOGY

I wrote a eulogy for the oak tree.

I knew every bird, animal and insect that lived in your branches and on your bark. For an hour every day; rain or shine, night or day, cold-snap or heat-wave, I climbed into your swaying branches, a sacred place. And I felt it when I rested within your protection: satori. I can't find the words to say how much you will be missed. I will always remember you.

And I left it on the oak tree's mighty stump where a little acorn lay. And in a blink of my eye, I spied, the brilliant blue flash of a jay.

LOCKDOWN

Do you remember the virus that spread like
wildfire through the numbered districts and
housing estates? It was very scary, wasn't it?
One inhabitant said it came from contaminated
drinking water. Another said it was the result of
a plague spread by rats. Others said it was
caused by an infestation of cockroaches, but no
one really knew why the virus started or what to
do about it.

People wore masks over their mouths and noses,
plastic gloves on their hands. Through the walls
of our small, stone cottage I smelt sickness and
horror and terror.

There was lockdown.

Through my writing room window, I watched the
ambulances long into the night, wailing sirens

and flashing blue lights. Bodies wrapped in blankets were taken away. In the space of a day one thousand and forty-six people died.

The workmen in florescent orange jackets and hard, white hats fumigated everywhere.
'We must find somewhere else to live.'
Jack was right but I said:
'I'm not leaving our small, stone cottage.'
'You owe it to Bel and me.'
I do not remember exactly what I said after that. The red mist came down. I brandished insults like broken bottles. Jack was silent, so were you. He left the room, so did you.

I was alone.

In the wild garden Jack had his head in his hands. You were by his side. I do not know what came over me:
'Playing the victim, are we?' I sneered, wanting him to answer back, but when he did, it simply

fueled my fury.

'I'm at my wits' end.'

'Poor Jack!' I mocked.

He did not say anything.

'Grow a backbone.'

I don't recall hitting him, but suddenly he was doubled over coughing and gagging. You with your arms around him, shouting:

'That was not fair, Mammy!'

And I moved to hold you, but you screamed at me:

'GO AWAY! I NEVER WANT TO SEE YOU AGAIN!'

NESTS & ACORNS

All was eerily quiet.

Jack was not lying beside me the next morning.

I got up.

You were not in your bed.

I went down the wooden ladder into the kitchen.

I saw a note on the big, wooden table:

I must put Bel first...

I did not read anymore.

I ran to the shed.

Jack was helping you into the truck.

He reached out to take the axe from me, but I wrong footed him and moved out of the way.

He spun round and round.

That was when I struck. I had no intention of hurting him. But he crashed to the ground, his bark splitting and peeling, leaves curling and burning, nests falling from his beard and hair, acorns tumbling from his ears and nose and mouth. As he exploded into a myth of himself. And you were nowhere to be seen.

I think that's what happened. I can't be sure. Even now there is so much I don't remember correctly. And as Mother said, 'Things are not always what they seem.'

VIXEN

Do you remember celebrating Samhain when we first lived at our small, stone cottage? Jack, you and I built the bonfire at the bottom of the wild garden, didn't we? And I explained to you, as Mother had explained to me, that we were entering the dark half of the year. The beginning of winter. A time when the harvest of our ancestors was in and the livestock were brought down from the summer pastures. A time when the Sun King was sacrificed back to the land with the seeds until his rebirth at the winter solstice. A time when the portal between this world and the Otherworld was open, a world as real as any other, a world of the imagination. A time for dreaming.

'Why do we have a bonfire, Mammy?'

'To make sure the light will return,' I replied as I lit a rag and threw it onto the kindling. A V of wild geese passed overhead.

The three of us stood hand- in-hand watching the flames leap into the air, listening to the wood crackling. Sitting on chairs round the fire, we ate the buttermilk bread I had baked and a stew prepared from vegetables grown in the wild garden. Jack and I drank elderberry wine. You sipped juice made from the apples we had pressed.

Later, when the flames died down, we scattered seeds over the ashes. Back inside our small, stone cottage, we let the darkness engulf us for a while. Eventually we lit candles in honour of our ancestors.

You fell asleep on my knee, one finger hooked over your nose, thumb in mouth wearing your dressing gown and rabbit slippers, dormouse-snug under Mother's quilted blanket. At midnight Jack picked you up and took you to bed.

This Samhain was so different.

I didn't light a bonfire or prepare a feast.

I didn't eat or sleep or wash or do anything
except think about you and Jack.

I thought I had struck Jack with the axe, but
maybe I had imagined it as I searched
everywhere but could not find him. Or you.

I stopped taking my pills. And spoke sharply to
myself,
'You will never go to that hell hole again.'

Each night I went to bed leaving the window
open for the visitations of my dreams, hoping to
receive a calling telling me where I could find
you, but it didn't. Instead I heard:
aham sah aham sah
And it was then, intuitively I knew, I had to
make a journey. Much as it pained me, it was
time to leave what I knew and venture into the
unknown. Our small, stone cottage must have

To Saul David

Foraging for insects and earthworms, pelt
catching sunlight, reddening to earth and copper,
tasting the air: bark, sap, mulch. My nose
twitched. My ears pricked. The fur lifted along
my spine. As I dropped to my haunches, leapt a
long leap. A flurry of dead leaves. A scuffle. The
excitement and fear a tangible taste on my
tongue. A squeal as I bit down hard on the
rabbit's neck, twisting it this way and that,
slurping hot blood. A savage snapping. I tore its
head clean off, cracked its skull with my molars.
Gorging richly on its brain, slashing the chest,
tearing the soft belly, spilling blubbery ropes of
purple and blue, scarlet too. I gobbled it all up,
then delicately licked myself clean.

Satiated, I curled under the roots of a yew tree,
smelling buds and leaves and the malty earth. A
clean, cold calm penetrated my bones. As I felt a
presence far larger than me, one which endured
in my memory. I blinked.

The morning hatched, yellowing the blue sky, waking it up with sunshine. There was the scent of dew and the sharp promise of a new day. The cotton bud tail of a deer bounded over a tree stump.

The vixen, on her paws, flicked her brush. In a flash she was off. Flickers of red-rust ignited by cloud breaks. I watched until she disappeared deep into the forest; it was then that I saw it glinting, partially hidden by leaf litter on the ground: the two tiny swans on a silver chain, the necklace Jack had given me in another life. I fastened it round my neck, sadness almost drowning me, but then I sensed her.

I reached out to touch her lovely, silver hair, but she was no longer there. And then I saw Jack and you in the bark of trees, in the bracken, but when I looked once more, you shifted into shadows, slowly slipping away, and then you too were gone. So, I plodded on, towards the river-that-runs-both-ways.

WISE-WOMAN

The wise-woman was fishing. She wore earth-
brown skirts and big boots. Eyes the colour of
vines. Face wrinkled as a pickled walnut. She
raised her hand in greeting. I did the same. Did
she know me from another life?

And I waited for her to offer me three wishes, but
she simply, nodded and gestured beyond the
river-that-runs-both-ways.

I looked in the direction she had pointed, but
when I turned back to thank her, she dissolved
into the forest.

I walked through dappled light, past beech and
silver birch trees and brambles and bushes,
pushing through dense thickets, stepping over
gnarled logs velveted with moss, tangles of ivy,
squishing and slipping and sliding along the
path, clogged and claggy with mud, following a

wren hopping from branch to branch, but then it
too disappeared. So, I took a track worn by deer,
lulled by distant soft flute sounds into a
labyrinth, spiraling into the centre, where I
thought I saw something not quite human,
and then I found myself back out again.

The sky was hardly visible through the canopy of
horse chestnut trees shaking their candelabras,
just flashes of blue hue, the sound of leaves
stirring in a breeze like someone blowing over
the top of a green bottle.

And what I breathed out, the trees breathed in,
what the trees breathed out, I breathed in.

A mauve-lilac mist rose from the ground,
bluebells singing their scent cut through with the
tang of lichen and wild garlic.   There was a
scattering of wood anemones, holding their faces
upwards to sunlight. There was the drumming of
a woodpecker. The *onk* of a nuthatch. It was

soft underfoot now. My steps made tiny squeaks on pine needles. Sometimes, colliding with fallen branches, I brushed past more ferns and more brambles snagging and pulling at my skirts.

Was that a wolf loping through the shadows? Yellow, full-moon eyes, grey pelt bristling, long tongue spooling from between its black lips? Or was I alone? I was not because when I looked closely, I saw that the forest was teeming with life and I was part of it, part of the connected planet.

It was as if my arms were branches, my fingers leaves. Feet rooted in mulch, slow sweet decay. Then I saw Jack. Tall and lithe as an oak sapling, but when I looked again, he vanished.

SEVEN STARS HILLS

The woods gave way to rocky terrain. In places
there was shingle, slippery, small landslides.
Feet scuffling as I climbed up cracks in the rocks.
Mother once said, I climbed like a mountain goat.

Leaning into the hot wind, I passed a rowan
growing out of a crevice, finally reaching the top
of one of the Seven Stars Hills. It was scattered
with grey-white rocks capped with purple
heather and gravel paths.   Below, the wind
raged over the land tearing into trees, shaking
their branches and leaves.
Suddenly, a voice was echoing around me:
'May! May! Collect as many flowers as you can
find and sew them into a gown.'
I don't know why I obeyed I just did.

Returning to the forest, I gathered as many wood
anemones as I could; each time I picked one,

another re-grew. When I finished stitching my
fingers were blistered and bleeding.

And then I saw it. The wild swan flying towards
me, her neck extended, her muscled wings
beating slowly:
aham sah aham sah
Immediately I threw the gown into the air and
pulled it over my head. There was a creaking
and cracking as my body twitched and scratched.
I hissed and flapped. My neck stretching out
from my breast. The silver chain breaking,
falling to the ground, as I opened and flexed my
immense wings, pushed off on grey webbed feet,
lifting myself into the sky.

Ethereal and weightless, outside time, in the air.
I swooped, then soared over the forest, Seven
Stars Hills and the river-that-runs-both-ways.
My senses acute. I heard water gurgling, leaves
rustling, insects hopping though the grass. And

when I turned my head, as the wild swan and I
flew side by side, I stared straight into her
forget-me-not blue eyes.

OM-A-U-M

There was an eerie hush.

Then I heard it.

The wind picking up, flattening the grass below,
a plectrum plucking branches, strumming leaves.
Trees simmering to boiling with rage.

A distant rumble, growing and expanding. A
roaring now, terrifying. Raw, angry energy,
rushing over the planet, out of control, all
encompassing.

Clouds raced in shifting colours: lavender, violet,
indigo, navy-blue. Deep cracks of thunder.
Forks of lightning shocking the sky silver.
Flinging flares of fury. Blinding my eyes. The
wind howling, wreaking havoc like something set
free from the underworld. Whipping and

whining, tearing at my

wings; still I beat them savagely, until I became

a swirling maelstrom of black sky and white

feathers.

All one cycle of complete connectedness clouds,

sky, swan and I searching for the path back to

the beginning

Then the rain came, the first rain for months and

months. Softly at first.

Odd spots

Here and

there

Here and

there

Then

harder the rain heavy falling in sheets drilling

into the dry earth

saying all it wanted to say

over and over

again

and nothing

and nobody

could stop

it

WHOOSH waves, sky high!

A surging sea of mud, snatching everything in its path: trees, bushes, brambles, sucking up the numbered districts, housing estates, distribution centres, parking zones, loading areas, fences, security gates, roads, shops, hotels, garages and pylons, waves, crashing and lashing and smashing.

The planet stopped turning.

Time moved/s in slow motion, forwards and backwards, to where there wa/is no past or future.

The planet started turning.

A cycle of earth, wind, air, fire and water.

And then the rain plopped and stopped speaking, drew in a deep breath, a swirling vapour of sounds.

All was still.

All was silent.

The sun came out.

Mist rose from the ground.

The water dried up.

There was land but she was barren and flat, nothing grew.

I was silence. I was stillness. And at that moment I was nothing but the moment.

It was a time that existed just below the surface:
malleable, half-awake.

Slowing down, I returned to my breath. As the
animate Earth spoke

A primordial vibration of the cosmos:

OM-A-U-M

REBIRTH

Believe me, Bel, when I say, I saw with my own
eyes. A change in energy. Something created
from nothing.

The earth contracted to the skies restlessly alive
yelling screaming bellowing wailing roaring
grunting giving birth to mountains rising like a
backbone from the plain rivers flowing winding
across the land cascading into waterfalls rushing
gushing oceans boulders and rocks wave upon
wave crashing to the shore kicking up dust
bearing down to the ground pushing up shoots
bursting into buds blooming into blossom singing
the names of things creating all life.

And as the wild swan flew into the distance, I
tumbled from the sky shift-shaping becoming the
human me, sitting beneath an oak tree. Slowly I
anchored myself to my breath to be: a leaf, a

branch, the tree.

It was then that I saw the swallows flying above sand dunes and mountains, crossing the ocean, exploding in spangles of sunlight, showing their royal-blue backs and scarlet throats. And I recalled Mother once saying to me,
'Everything is connected.'

Suddenly sunshine burst from the beak of a song thrush and it sang with joy in an intricate layer of sound,
'Once you choose hope anything is possible.'
So, I put my ear to the land to hear its story. I heard its slow, steady breathing. And then it spoke to me, in music of damp earth and prophecies of rain, whistles of feathers and scents of birdsong, tastes of wildflowers and saw-toothed leaves. And all the while two little words fell like seeds onto fertile ground. Eventually, I picked up a twig and scratched in the soil what

the land had told me:

It is time for a new beginning, a new way of thinking, a new way of living. It is time for change.

Just then, the kin flew overhead and disappeared over ki backwards towards the river-that-runs-both-ways. And I followed.

AFTERWORD

Even as a child I was a lover of wild things. I lived in Meadow Avenue on the edge of Priesty Fields where I spent most of my out-of-school time exploring the natural world. I was never happier than when I was tramping through fields and splashing in streams, swimming in rivers and building dens.

Fast forward fifty years.

I live in Haslington, a village nestling between the railway town, Crewe, and the market town, Sandbach. When we first moved to the village it was a biodiversity hotspot. That changed when the developers muscled in with their diggers and chainsaws. Within weeks land was gobbled up.

Trees uprooted. Streams damned. Fields churned up into piles of earth. Habitats trashed.

The biodiversity hotspot was (almost) gone. Luckily the wood remains. It is a place I walked before the virus with my springer spaniel, Sophie, but I had not been there since she died.

The first night of lockdown I dream about the wood. I dream about Sophie. And wake longing to go there.

The sun, golden as a buttercup, shines from a cloudless, cornflower-blue sky. My heart thumps in my chest as I close our front door behind me. Hurrying along the road which normally would be busy with children dawdling to school, people jogging or walking their dogs before work, but this is the *new* normal. And there is only me.

The village school is silent. Blinds are down at the pub on Fox Corner. The shop and post office are closed. Outside the pharmacy people are silently queuing round the car park, two metres' distance, wearing masks. It's eerie like a scene from an apocalyptic film. My thoughts are racing.

My breathing erratic. I am sprinting now. But when I turn onto the track and climb over the stile, I stop.

This is a world steeped in green. In a faint breeze, the grass rises and falls like waves. I smell its zinginess, taste its freshness on my tongue. And when I look up and see swallows flashing like bright needles embroidering the sky, something shifts in me and I slip into another reality. For the first time in days, I feel completely calm.

The ash trees are studded with sticky, black buds. A parliament of rooks gather in untidy, twiggy nests, flapping their ragged wings, cawing. Then I notice them, peeping shyly through a scatter of leaf litter, I crouch to observe closely, *Primula vulgaris*, primroses, my

Mother's favourite flower.

Although I rarely take photographs, I am compelled to take one of the primroses on my phone.

I venture into the woods, the spirit of Sophie at my side. Branches are overhanging, knotted with ivy, a place of shifting patterns of light-shade. There is a rich scent of damp earth and leaves. Shoots of bluebells thrust their way through mulch. My heart is thumping again, but in a good way now. As I come across a bridal train of star-bright wood anemones, lacy leaves, dusky pink petals on the outside. I take a photograph and scribble notes in my journal. I am slowing down, paying full attention, finding my way back to myself.

When I arrive home, I post the photographs of the primroses and wood anemone on my *Facebook* page. Within minutes there is a response that both surprises and delights me; clearly, like me, people are finding joy and solace in the natural world.

That evening I hear on the news how the *Wildlife Trusts* are recording huge numbers of people tuning into their webcams. Many people across the country are sharing images of the natural world. Locked in, we tune into digital platforms: live streaming, images and video blogs to experience the magic of wild things. *Biophilia*, the intense human need we have to connect with the wider natural world during times of crisis; in wild things we see hope.

If Covid-19 has shown us anything, it's shown us we're not in control. The planet is a complex, finely balanced web of interconnections. Everything is related to everything else. Nothing is separate. Everything has its own integral part to play. If something is taken away everything shifts and changes.

Throughout 2020, the natural world has soothed and sustained us, filled us with wonder and hope. It has been here for us during our hour of need. Ki and kin now need us. It is time to have 'a change of mindset, attitude and behaviour. If we feel it, we must be galvanized by our ecological grief' to protect all life: rivers, mountains, trees, flowers, creatures, for, make no bones about it, planet Earth is the place we all call home.

ACKNOWLEDGEMENTS

My gratitude goes to those who have been part of
my quest to write this book.

I thank my *Facebook* friends who have shared
my joy in the natural world, spring, 2020. Thank
you to Shelley Aspden and Dan Octon for sharing
my essay: *It's Time For Change* with the
Ministry Of Yoga community. And thanks to
Lucy Jones for her generosity in permitting me to
quote from her book, *Losing Eden*. Huge thanks
are due to Jo Thilwind for kindly writing a
wonderful foreword. Her passion and energy for
the natural world are amazing. I wish to thank
Wild Woman, Jill Amison, for adventures into
magical landscapes and yoga workshops
brimming with compassion and joy. And Julie
Miles, my loyal friend, who reads my writing
with a big heart and generous spirit. Geoff
Sutton and Dr Jenny Newman, my Creative

Writing tutors many years' ago, inspired me so much: thank you. And thank you to my parents, Kathleen and Vincent Armstrong for encouraging my love of the natural world from when I was a child. I'm forever grateful to my editor, Dr Meriel Lland, who has accompanied me on this journey. I'm indebted to Meriel for her time, patience, encouragement and enthusiasm. Thank you so much for your insight, sensitivity and for being there. From the bottom of my heart, I thank Dr Dave Colton; his beautiful art work adorns the cover of this book. I am grateful to Dave, for once again, helping me make my dreams come true. And to the small, stone cottage, La Paperie, Cousmes Vauce: 1990-2012, a very special thank you.

Printed in Poland
by Amazon Fulfillment
Poland Sp. z o.o., Wrocław

65765515R00115